What they are saying about
Who is God When We Hurt?

What I love about Scibienski's memoir is that it's not primarily her own—through the interweaving stories of her late husband, her family, her community of faith, and her own vulnerable struggle as a pastor to know and trust God, we come face to face with our own questions, trials, challenges, and fears. It is a memoir that straddles the boundaries between narrative and devotional: inviting and enticing us through even the most painful of stories to know and trust that God is already and always a part of all our stories, too.

Rev. Dr. Erin Raffety
Lecturer, Practical Theology
Princeton Theological Seminary

Beth's book features compassion—both to those facing unspeakable heartache, and to Beth herself who lived with sometimes unbearable heartache. Beth points us to faith and shows us that God doesn't disappear during our difficulties. Instead, God shows up stronger to sit and stand with us. A must-read for anyone who questions how they will continue when life feels too difficult.

Denise M. Brown
Founder
CareGiving.com

In Who Is God When We Hurt?, Beth speaks directly from her heart to the heart of the reader. Although she is writing about her own experience in caring for her husband Pete she is speaking for so many other caregivers traveling that same path and facing those same challenges. Who Is Go When We Hurt? is a sweet, compelling, and honest telling of what it means to be a caregiver, the value of community, and how we all need each other. Thank you, Beth, for the courage to tell your story, including the challenges of caregiving and of faith.

Elissa Lewin

Founder and Executive Director
Nancy's House: Caring for Caregivers

Who is God when we hurt? Listen to the pastor, the caregiver. Listen to Beth—for this book reveals a completely human character on every page. A woman who is unafraid, or simply willing to be foolish enough to speak honestly, to ask impossible questions, to refuse to let go, and then to model for all of us how to let go. It's not Rev. Scibienski's bravery that most captures the reader—and there is much of that in this book—it's her quirky humanity—and that of her husband, her sons, her congregants, and friends—a humanity that lifts every reader into a conversation both pained and elegant. Reading this book, every single one of the fifty-plus essays and poems, is like sitting with a friend, a friend who remains through the trauma when everything feels fragile and things are out of control. She does not shout at us from the sidelines. An honest, healing book with human fingerprints all over it, a book that dares to follow the guidance of one's anger and to ask the unaskable questions. This book affords a healing therapy for anyone who is ready, or almost ready, to ask the questions.

Dr. Virgnia Wiles
Professor of New Testament
New Brunswick Theological Seminary

WHO IS

GOD

WHEN WE

HURT?

*A Pastor-Caregiver
wrestles with
grief, loss, faith,
& doubt*

BETH SCIBIENSKI

Open Door Publications

Who Is God When We Hurt?
A Pastor-Caregiver wrestles with grief, loss, faith & doubt

ISBN: 978-1-7328202-0-3

Published by
Open Door Publications
2113 Stackhouse Dr.
Yardley, PA 19067
www.OpenDoorPublications.com

Cover Design: Eric Labacz, www.labaczdesign.com

*For Pete
and the Saints of
Grace Presbyterian Church*

TABLE OF CONTENTS

PROLOGUE
I PROMISE

EACH TIME I OFFICIATE A WEDDING, I find myself renewing my own wedding vows. Those of us who choose to live in a community such as a church experience life exponentially. We go to that many more weddings, that many more funerals; we witness that many more births, and that many more children growing up before our eyes. One year, our church community had seven funerals! On any given Sunday we pray for at least seven people who are severely ill! We live with an extended family of sorts—riding the wave of life's encounters together. Up and down, around we go.

When we experience the ups and downs of another person's life, we are invited to evaluate our own ups and downs. As the pastor of a church, I am always amazed at how much I have learned about grief and illness by being in relationship with so many others riding the waves of life. If I look back, I have learned many lessons about job loss, financial burdens, and the reimagining of one's future. I have witnessed many other couples learning how to love, how to commit, and watched people wrestle with their vows.

There is a moment in every wedding when a wave of emotion travels from my heart up through my spine and tries desperately to fill my eyes with tears. It is the moment when the happy couple says, "I promise to love you...in sickness and in health."

What do any of us know of the vows we take in marriage? In the same way we can't really be ready for the important things of life, we can't possibly know what "to love in sickness and in health" means. And the truth is—we don't need to. Sometimes I wonder about the people who wrote those traditional vows. What was going on in their lives? What had they witnessed that had them fashion those words as they are? If I were tasked with writing wedding vows in an official wedding book, would I include words like that? If not that, what would I write?

Pete and I did not use the traditional language in our vows. We wrote our vows after the prayer attributed to St. Francis entitled "Make me an instrument of thy peace." We vowed to sow love where there was hatred, hope where there was despair, light where there was darkness. We vowed to console, to understand, and to die to ourselves. We had no idea what we were talking about! And yet, the words fit us so very well. If I had to write an official book of vows now, having witnessed what I've witnessed, having officiated what I've officiated, I might include something like this:

I, NAME, take you, NAME, to be my partner in life.
To share the happenings of life every day—
the mundane along with the profound.
I promise to spend my gifts and resources
to build a life together, physically, emotionally, and
spiritually.
I promise to love my children, your children, our children.
And when we are poor,
or when we lose jobs,
or when we get sick,
or when the creek rises...

Yeah, no one is gonna ask me to write an official book with vows in it anyway. What would you promise? What are we supposed to promise?

At this time in our relationship, I had begun to feel that the best promise I could make would be to remain. I will remain with Pete, my husband. I will remain with my family. I will remain with those under my care as a pastor. Sometimes I will be fully engaged. Sometimes I will be a depressed, raggedy woman. Sometimes I will have a great sense of humor, and sometimes my anxiety will be so palpable that I'm going to need you to help me breathe. I will remain and, in promising to remain, I promise that I will change. We will not be who we are the day we promised.

Pete and I changed so much. We made promises at one

moment in time. Tangible, recordable, legal promises that also helped us evolve. Our promises weren't immutable. They rode the waves of life with us.

I remember standing before this lovestruck couple as they uttered the words, "in sickness and in health," and I wanted to say, "Are you sure? Do you really want to say that out loud? Because you're going to change. Everything that you experience together or apart is going to affect you, and how you think you'll keep this promise is not how you really will. And how you think this promise will be tested...well, you simply can't fathom." Of course, I didn't say that out loud. And it's not that I wanted to dissuade them from making that promise. In fact, what I was really thinking is, they can't possibly know the kind of wave that may hit them. None of us can.

Control

As part of my preparation for becoming a pastor, I completed a field education assignment as a chaplain at an urban hospital. The hospital was designated a Trauma 1 Center. One of the first things I learned in the orientation for this assignment was the definition of "trauma." Trauma is damage by an external force. That's it. Trauma can be a car accident or a gunshot wound. Trauma can be a fist to the jaw or a head hitting the concrete driveway after falling off a ladder. When one thing strikes another there is trauma.

When someone comes to the hospital because of trauma it is called a Code 40. I was told it was called that because 40 personnel are called to the scene. One of the 40 is the chaplain. Over the loudspeaker we would hear the code announced, "Code 40—by ambulance," for example. That meant the person who had experienced a trauma is headed to the hospital by ambulance. Often, those words would follow with further instructions letting us know how many minutes they believed it would be before the patient arrived at the hospital.

One balmy spring night, I responded to a Code 40, an urban brawl that ended in a knife injury. The factions of the brawl followed the ambulance to the emergency room, the anger led the way. One sunny, Saturday afternoon, I responded to a young woman in a motorcycle accident. As the surgeons worked on her mangled body, I attended to her husband, a burly, tattooed hulk-of-a-guy who fell into my arms weeping. He had watched the trauma happen—his wife lost control of her motorcycle and slid onto the pavement going 50 miles per hour. One winter morning, I consoled an aging wife whose husband had climbed a ladder to affix Christmas lights to their home. Trauma by fall. And one spring evening, a trauma call over the loudspeaker woke me—Code 40 by ambulance, five minutes.

I opened my eyes, looked around my on-call bedroom. One bed, a television, and a small desk with a chair. I turned on the lamp by my bed, quickly dressed, and made my way to the trauma section of the emergency room. A few of my colleagues had already gathered: residents, patient advocates, security officer, surgeons. The trauma was a car accident. The driver of the vehicle, a teenager, was wheeled into the room where the frenzied trauma activity began, at least 12 people monitoring different things, each responsible for a unique part of this young man's care. The passenger of the car was dead on arrival. Neither of their families were present. The security officer began going through the young man's belongings, the patient advocate logged each item: $13, a driver's license, and then a note. The guard opened it up, began to read but then looked up for me, "Are you the chaplain?" "Mm-humm," nodding my head. He handed me the note.

I began to read a scratched out note that laid clear intentions of a suicide pact. I took a deep breath and looked up to find four residents standing over my shoulders reading the note. I stopped reading to notice the reactions of the physicians. I asked, "Hey, you ok?" At first they didn't say anything. They didn't even really want to look at me. As the chaplain, I represent all of the things that are out of their control. Physicians are taught and trained to repair life, to control bleeding, to help others escape death. When life isn't repaired, or bleeding persists, or death wins, the chaplain is called. Usually I didn't force myself into their world but I couldn't let it go this time.

"Seriously, are you okay?"

One finally spoke, "It pisses me off."

"Yes," I say, "I imagine it would."

Another spoke up, "Stupid kid, he writes the damn note and he survives while his friend dies. What's he gonna do now?"

Then another added, "Why should we save him? He wanted to die. Look at all that's going on to save him right now." We all looked up and into the trauma room.

After this pause, I returned to the note to read it again. I asked if anyone was calling his parents and arranged to be in the ER when they arrived. I folded up the note and handed it back to the officer on duty. "Thanks," I said with closed lips and sad eyes.

I take a moment for myself, go upstairs to the lobby where there is a water fountain and a gas fireplace with comfortable chairs. The lobby is empty in the middle of the night and I pick a good seat to catch my breath and gather my thoughts. What would I feel if this was my child? What would I think if this was my child? I try to imagine what will happen when he wakes. He will be greeted by a team of psychologists all wanting to help him find health. Will he want that? How will his parents convince him to want that? What relationship will his parents have with the grieving parents of the friend who died? Who will have to do this funeral? Thank God it's not me. Of course that same clergy might eventually say, "Thank God I wasn't the chaplain on call for this one." What scripture might I use? Should I use scripture here? What can I pray if they ask me to pray? If they don't ask, should I offer to pray?

Those questions are typical and expected but not always helpful. Providing care for people happens in the moment, face to face, or voice to voice. I hadn't yet met the parents. And often all those questions are not helpful because like this night, the psychologists and social workers got to the parents before me, and although physicians told them I was available, I didn't meet them until 7 a.m. the next morning. By this time, their son was resting in a room in the Pediatric Emergency Unit. He would be transferred to a facility soon; he sustained few physical injuries.

I knocked lightly on the door and saw the parents on either side of the bed while a physician checked his vitals. The mother thanked me for coming. She asked if I had seen the note. I nodded.

"Do you have the note?" I asked.

"Yes." And after a pause, she said, "We don't understand."

"I imagine you wouldn't; be kind to yourself with this."

She wiped tears from her eyes. I touched her shoulder and told her I had been thinking and praying for her all night. I had prayed for strength and wisdom, and now I would pray for kindness. She thanked me. I told her that I was about to go off call but there was always a chaplain on call and that I would pass on the information so that someone could check in with them later. I turned around and walked away. I returned to my bedroom, packed up my things, and after checking in with the pastoral care office, I went home.

It was not quite gray. The sun was shining through the wispy clouds here and there. There was a slight breeze. I watched as the world began to wake up—a woman walked on the sidewalk, a store owner put out a rack of shirts. When I arrived home, I made coffee and found a place on the couch to stare out the window for awhile. What had just happened? A person tried to take his own life; a person was unsuccessful in trying to take his own life. A person took a friend's life. Parents lost a son, whom they had spent endless energy keeping alive for over a decade—feeding, bathing, protecting, clothing, teaching, nurturing, loving, maybe even kissing and hugging. Another set of parents found a broken son. What was his childhood like? Did they take him to karate lessons, swimming lessons, piano lessons? Band concerts? Soccer games? Did they have to help with math homework? Starting that morning, those parents began a new chapter in their parenting journey. They were now raising a son who unsuccessfully tried to take his own life.

This traumatic experience lived with me amidst my class schedule and family activities. I didn't notice any signs of post trauma; I didn't appear to have any triggers from it. It's not that I could not stop thinking about it. But I would say I was reminded of it often. Three months later I came to understand why it was lingering beneath the surface of my mind: control. We fully lack control in this life. As I said before, as the chaplain (and possibly now as a pastor), I represented all of the things that are out of our control. The chaplain, the pastor, is available to talk about life when life is not making sense, when life is frightening, when life is—out of our control. As a pastor, I have a front row seat for all that is fragile in life; I am present when life is untenable. The majority of conversations that I have had with people, as a chaplain and as a pastor, dance around the truth that the world is unsafe.

Now trauma in the hospital is more obvious. We know when damage has been done by an external force. But trauma is not limited to car accidents and gunfire. Trauma is anything that disrupts. Trauma is anything that stops us in our tracks. In the parish, I have responded to trauma that comes in the form of divorce, diagnosis, death. We lack control. The world is indeed unsafe. We live in fear. I live in fear. I was living in some residual fear from this experience in the hospital with this young man who unsuccessfully tried to end his life.

And this unsuccessful attempt turned control on its head for me. Most of the trauma, the lack of control I was tending to, was about stopping bad from happening. But this young man tried to create bad—attempted to create a traumatic event that would result in death—and he was unsuccessful. That failed attempt at trauma was in itself traumatic for him. He was heading in a direction of destruction, and his plan was disrupted. My mind was wandering in and out of this experience, grappling with the reality that we are neither in control of saving our lives, nor are we in control of taking our lives.

Shortly after my stint as a chaplain I was ordained in the Presbyterian Church (USA) and began working with a small church in central New Jersey. Two years into this pastorate a beloved member of my congregation was diagnosed with ALS. Her good friend and I were sharing a bottle of wine in her kitchen.

I sit across from this woman—she sports a stylish, short, platinum blonde haircut and she wears sandals way before Easter and well into the fall. She has been an elder for years; she has a deep passion for justice in our world and has developed a variety of opportunities for our congregation to serve hurting, broken people in our community. I have grown to trust her, her heart, and her ministry.

I ask, "How are you doing with your friend's illness?" She gathers tears in her eyes, finds a tissue, and says, "I don't know why I bother with mascara anymore," as it runs down her face. After a pause and bite of shrimp, she starts again, "It's hard, it's really hard. She had already suffered with the breast cancer."

She sniffs, blinks and finds her forceful voice to say, "And she fought hard, she won that battle with cancer. And now look; I can't bear to see her suffer like this."

I finish chewing and say, "How can I help you through this?"

This woman has lived through more loss than anyone I have known. She buried three husbands. She lost her mother to Alzheimer's and a close friend to lymphoma. She has quilted together an incredible family from the broken pieces of three families. She loves them, and they love her. She is grandma in her own unique way while always honoring the other grandmothers involved. When she cries, her tears come in every color of grief.

Therein lies the beauty of grief: It is colorful. The tears she shed for her friend that afternoon leaked into tears shed for her husbands, that then leaked into tears for her mother. She said, "I thought Alzheimer's was the worst until I came face to face with ALS. This is worse."

"Yes, I believe so," I said.

"I don't ever want to go through this. And I won't. I don't think I've told you this yet but I'm going to take my life if I ever get Alzheimer's disease."

Looking up from my glass of wine, I say, "I'm sorry; what?"

"I might as well tell you now, Jean (her friend with ALS) and I have spoken about suicide at length. We've even purchased this book. I will lend it to you when I finish. It's all about how to kill yourself...and did you know that none of the options are ever really fool-proof? The author suggests that you always put a bag over your head just in case your first choice doesn't work."

I have no idea what facial expression I had at that moment. I remember taking a deep breath, putting a smile on my face, stopping to pour another glass of wine, and if I remember correctly, I said, "Stop, just for a second." She laughed with her wonderful chuckle, shaking her head at me, a youngster pastor whom she had grown to love and need. "Start over," I ask. "The two of you are talking about suicide?"

"Well, we've talked about it but I don't think she'll be able to do it. She's always been such a good, Christian girl. But we've been looking into which pills she is taking and how she could collect some on the side."

After a sip of wine she continued, "The thing that makes me most mad is that there isn't assisted suicide in New Jersey. I told her, 'I love you but I'm not going to jail. You're going to have to do this on your own. I'll be there with you, but I can't help you do it.'"

"What did she say to that?" I asked.

"She agreed and also laments that there is no assisted suicide in New Jersey. If there was, this would not be an issue. She would be able to talk to her physician about her wishes. The problem with ALS is that by the time it's too much for her to handle, she won't be able to do it herself. She'll be too weak or she'll have lost the use of her arms or even her voice." We paused and looked at one another.

Now my mind was spinning—I certainly didn't want someone in my church to have thoughts of suicide. While I had personal preferences and political beliefs about it, I had not anticipated this conversation. My pastoral training certainly didn't cover this. Any psychological training I had told me that thoughts of suicide are signs of disease, severe signs of an unhealthy mind. In the abstract, this conversation needed to be shared with a professional. But then I realized she *was* sharing this with a professional. I was that professional. I knew my role as a pastor, and this conversation was most certainly meant for her pastor. I was her pastor. So the words I chose had nothing to do with my personal preference or political beliefs about assisted suicide. The words I found had to do with relationship. I said, "Well, I don't think anyone should die alone. So, if the day comes, I want to be there."

She responded with concerns for me professionally. "I don't think you can. You'd be committing professional suicide. You would get into a lot of trouble for this, don't you think?" We went on to talk about how much involvement I could have if a congregant decided to end his or her life. Here we were, trying to control what is out of our control. A meandering conversation about life and death, illness and friendship, all of it trying to manage, or control, that which is out of our control. The conversation in my mind, however, was less about suicide and more about wondering how much control we have in the first place. Would her friend have enough control to end her life before her ALS progressed? Would she be able to control whether or not she lived with Alzheimer's disease?

What about the guy who ended up with a knife wound on that spring night? How much control did he think he had? Or what of the woman in the motorcycle accident or her husband who tried to warn her of the danger ahead? Did they have control? How much control? Sometimes it appears we are successful in saving a life through machinery or medicine. Other times we are unsuccessful when we try to destroy life with a moving car and a note to our parents. Life is filled with trauma, and we are not in control.

Casting Out a Line

My husband Pete and I were walking back to our car after attending a Bonnie Raitt concert at the State Theater in downtown New Brunswick, New Jersey. Pete first saw Bonnie Raitt in concert when he only 18. She was about the same age at the time, not yet famous. He had had a little crush on her ever since. Midway through the concert that evening, she surprised us by inviting Rock and Roll hall of famer, Grammy winner and beloved session musician, Dr. John, onto the stage. Although Pete didn't show it, I knew he was thrilled.

I had been listening to her music in preparation for the concert. One song I had been stuck on was "God Was in the Water." She played it that evening. The tune has a haunting melody. With her low, slow drawl she sang these words that rested like steam over the music, *Castin' out a line, Castin' out a line to the shadows, Castin' out a line but no one's biting.*

As we walked back to the car, I noticed that Pete was dragging his feet. "Pick up your feet," I said. Nag, nag, nag. He seemed to be a little slower than usual. Normally, Pete ambled. He really belonged in South Carolina, but the stork dropped him in central New Jersey. Pete spoke with a drawl. Maybe that's why he liked Bonnie Raitt. I nagged again, "Pick up your feet. Do you see that you're dragging a foot? Are you okay?" He replied, "Yeah, just a little tired, I guess." I wasn't ready for him to be tired. I was 18 years younger than Pete. I wasn't ready to slow down. But there I was on Livingston Avenue, slowing down to see what was wrong with Pete and his dragging foot.

We had turned the corner and settled into our white Honda Accord when I asked the oddest thing of him. "Honey, try something for me. Lift your right knee. Now your left. And your right again." By the third round, he was unable to lift his right leg. He looked at me, "Well, that's odd." "Yeah," I said.

I turned the key and headed home. We didn't speak but Bonnie Raitt was ringing in my head, *Castin' out a line, Castin' out a line to the shadows, Castin' out a line but no one's biting.*

We made an appointment to see our primary care doctor/internist, thinking that he probably had pulled something or overexerted a muscle in his back. Physical therapy was going to be the answer, we were sure. I had been going to this doctor's office since I was a teenager. Our physician is Asian American, with a great smile and an even better laugh. She listens with her eyes. She agreed about sending Pete to physical therapy. We seemed content. But then something other than my logical mind spoke up and said, "But I hear a change in his speech pattern, too." Full stop. "You do?" she asked. "Yes, I do. I think something else might be going on with him?" I said, not knowing where it was coming from. Was I making it up? Why? What data did I have to support a theory other than a pulled muscle?

I don't have an answer to that question. Sometimes I think my subconscious simply overcame my conscious. A knowing within me took over and acted on my behalf. My subconscious had cast out a line and caught a script for an MRI and a referral to a neurologist.

Nonspecific white matter. There was *nonspecific white matter* in Pete's brain and spinal cord. We wanted our internist to read the MRI to us first. We would go to a neurologist but, wanted to hear her voice first. We trusted her. She knew us. "I'm sorry. It reads like multiple sclerosis. Go see the neurologist. There is treatment. He will know what to do now."

The first neurologist spoke to us as if he was unaware that he was making human contact. It wasn't just the medical terms that we didn't understand. He talked to us as if we were in the same science lab, doing an experiment together and preparing to write up a report. He didn't understand the basic definition of trauma. He didn't understand that the information he was reading on Pete's MRI was an external source, and it was hitting us— physically, emotionally, spiritually, mentally, relationally. He was delivering trauma. When I started to cry, he honestly looked surprised by my reaction. He seemed to take note of it as if he was keeping a file on "odd human behavior." After staring at me in confusion, he excused himself "to give us some privacy."

Pete looked like he had been kicked in the chest, the wind knocked out of him. I sat in the corner of the exam room trying unsuccessfully to stop crying. The doctor returned, and he said things. Non-specific white matter. Multiple sclerosis. Interferon injection treatment. Chronic, progressive disease.

We tried to listen but honestly, we needed to get out of there as fast as we could. *Castin' out a line, Castin' out a line to the shadows, Castin' out a line but no one's biting.*

He wrote a script, we made a follow-up appointment, and then we headed for our car with Pete's foot dragging behind.

Doctors and specialty pharmacies became part of our lives. Medication began to arrive at our back door in a cooler marked "refrigerate upon arrival." Pete began to take medicine that created false targets for his body to attack rather than his body attacking itself. *Castin' out a line, Castin' out a line to the shadows, Castin' out a line but no one's biting.*

One test led to another test that led to seeing another doctor that necessitated more tests, more medication, and more follow-up visits. We had experienced trauma; we were hit by an external force. With each test, pill, and physician, we were casting out a line. We were looking for something that would bring control back to the chaos. We were searching for the right treatment that would bring order and understanding to the diagnosis. We were trying to organize, manage, or control the trauma. Sometimes some piece of information would surface that made us feel as though we had "caught" some form of control on the line we had cast. Sometimes medicine would feel as if we had caught some relief. Pete would walk lighter…but still drag his foot.

People sent us articles and websites to read. Everyone else had more energy to attack Pete's diagnosis than either of us did. We hadn't recovered from the first kick in the chest. We moved very slowly into this reality, barely walking, really. We simply didn't want to create a relationship with multiple sclerosis (MS). Although working on treatments and thinking about alternative medicine or diet were needed, it felt as if we were giving away our life to MS. And no matter how we tried to engage with medicine and doctors and articles, we felt as if MS always had the upper hand. MS was in control; we were not.

Each time I surfed the internet for information about MS or treatment options, I was met with suffocating trauma. MS was hitting me over and over. I cried. All the time. My tears were casting out a line. Nothing, no one was biting.

Marco Polo

THERE ARE FISTFULS OF CLICHÉS THAT PEOPLE SAY in times of trauma. "When we are at the end of our rope, we are closest to God." "God never gives us more than we can handle." "When we are at our weakest, God is strong for us." Or how about the "Footprints" poem: "My child, when you see only one set of footprints, it was there where I carried you." And for many, these sayings provide great comfort. For many others, these sayings provoke a reaction of anger at what comes across as insensitivity to trauma.

The thing about God is that people have a very personal understanding and relationship with Him. For some, God is around each and every corner. I have a friend who believes that God helps her put her earrings on each morning. Every time she mentions it I think about the idiot who didn't hold the piercing gun straight and thus made it hard for her to put her earrings in every day. But the actual anatomy of her ear piercing isn't part of her narrative. For her, she asks God to help with her earrings, and God doesn't let her down. God helps.

For many others, God is not so reliable. Brought up by Bible-believing parents, we went to church every week without argument. God has been part of my life for as long as I can remember. Sometimes God has been as real and as reliable as the sunrise. At other times God has seemed distant, almost hidden. And for the times in between, I have found God in conversation, in silence, in books, in friendship, in cooking, in laughter, and so often in places where I wasn't looking.

Finding God amidst our daily lives is almost like exercise to me. It doesn't come easy. It requires thinking and muddling through confusion. I appreciate a good workout. But a good workout wears you out. A good workout should be followed by some nourishment. Exercise makes us thirsty. Some days I'd rather skip it altogether. Some days I drag my body to exercise just the way I drag my faith to God. Some days I'm tired. Some days I'm slower.

After Pete's diagnosis of MS, my faith was tired. Looking for God was both exhausting and lonely. My faith was slowing down, and I thought I might take a break from trying to find God. My faith wasn't damaged. My mortal soul was not in any danger. I had changed. My experiences had changed me, and my faith had changed with them. The past ways of understanding, interacting, and searching for God needed to change, too. But I was tired.

My sister-in-law, Elizabeth has a term for life events like the one I was going through. She calls them "qualifying events." A qualifying event is whenever we are changed as a result of walking through a life experience. If we make it through, if we learn, change, grow, adjust accordingly, we are then qualified to keep going in the game of life. As if we've "leveled up."

People go through qualifying events all the time. One winter weekday I watched a wealthy, successful businessman come through brain surgery, his face dripping with gratitude. Yet another winter weekday, a woman stood beside her husband's hospital bed. He had suffered a heart attack, and his brain had gone without oxygen for ten minutes before the EMT had arrived. Now we stood beside her as she decided whether to stop treatment.

Qualifying events provoke questions such as "Why did God let this happen?" When people are experiencing a qualifying event I hear things like "This doesn't seem fair." And "Where is God anyway?" When people are asking those questions of me, the pastor, I look for appropriate, loving ways to find God in them, in the room, in the experience. During qualifying events, during trauma, people are less interested in the theoretical understanding of God, and more interested in the presence of God. When we experience trauma, we recognize that things are really out of our control, and in response, we look for presence. We care less about what God is and more about where God is.

It is during times of trauma when we are most wanting God's presence. Trauma causes us to look for God, assuming God must be here somewhere. We need God to be present because we don't want to be alone, particularly when we are hurting. We look for God close to us—not in textbooks or in metaphysics. We don't ask philosophical questions. God is personal, not academic. The search for God, as I have seen, is more about making meaning than it is about finding faith. People know that the answer to "Where is God when it hurts?" is not simple. (If it was, then quite frankly, God may not be worth searching for. The search for what holds life together shouldn't be finished before suppertime, if you know what I mean.) God is not a simple concept. If there is a God, it most likely is something stronger or stranger than we can think of. If there is a God, then it is hopefully something infinitely more creative than the human mind and/or heart can conceive. Therefore, trying to wrap our heads around where God is—or isn't—can't be consolidated into an answer that fits on a bumper sticker...but oh, how I have tried.

For me, as a Christian person, the search for God almost always starts with scripture. I'm a "person of the book," as they say. But the book does not stand alone for me. God has been and continues to be revealed in as many ways as there are people. God, whatever that is, can be understood in a new way every day. The question "Where is God?" helps us to then interpret life. For me, the search for God involves mixing together scripture, nature, experiences, relationships, conversations, logic, and history until we find understanding and perhaps even make meaning out of life.

There were plenty of times during this early diagnosis of MS when the answer to "Where is God in this for me?" was "I don't know." I didn't like that answer, but it was the only one I had. I wanted to take a second (or third) look at what was happening to me, in me, around me. I wanted to squint sometimes. I wanted to gaze other times. I wanted to close my eyes and imagine.

We had experienced a qualifying event, and we were changed. The trauma changed how we perceived everything around us. Roads we always took to work seemed strange. Weekly, mundane tasks were supposed to provide comfort and stability. But after trauma, everything was different. Places that were safe no longer were. Old hiding places disappeared.

Living through trauma, making it through a qualifying event, wasn't simple. We are complex beings; my body, my mind, my spirit took me on rides I could not have imagined. I tried to listen to myself, to my inside self, during this first season of diagnosis. But searching for understanding, for truth, wasn't comfortable or comforting. Instead, I wanted to find where God was so that I could at least have God's presence with me.

Two of my sisters are almost the same age. Growing up, Kristin lived in New Jersey with Mom, and Tara lived in Texas with Dad. They spent the summers together, which required Kristin flying into Dallas-Fort Worth Airport. Upon arrival, she would listen for Tara who yelled "Marco." She would stay close to the gate until she heard it, and when she did she would respond with "Polo."

I tried to picture their 3-1/2 feet tall bodies searching for one another through crowds of people. I love the image of two tiny creatures ducking in and out of the sea of legs and luggage searching for one another. In my mind's eye I see Kristin with her curly hair carrying a Beverly Hills 90210 backpack, listening. I see Tara, already sun-kissed and glowing; I can hear her yelling "Marco." And I can see Kristin's smile and feel her joy as she responded with "Polo!" They searched with what they had, with what they were given.

And so did I—I searched for God, for meaning, for peace of mind with what I had. Pete and I had experienced trauma, we had received an unwanted diagnosis. We had gone through a qualifying event. We had changed. But I searched for God with what I had, wondering if I were to yell "Marco," would God respond with "Polo?"

Interpretation Stew

THE SEARCH FOR GOD IS ABOUT INTERPRETATION. It's about asking questions and reflecting on the answers. It's about letting one question lead to another and then another. I was taught to interpret where and what God is through interpreting the stories in the Bible. The Bible is filled with stories about people like you and me, and they're written by people like you and me—each of them searching for God, interpreting God in their own context. Fingerprints are all over these stories: The fingerprints of the ones who wrote the stories, the fingerprints of the ones who copied the words from one animal skin to another, one parchment to another. There is so much in these stories to uncover, unwrap, exhume even.

When I got married, I wore my mother's wedding dress. The dress was preserved. Unwrapping it was like exhuming the dead. There were three layers of vacuum-packed plastic to cut through. It was preserved with the purpose of survival but getting to it made me realize that it wasn't necessarily preserved with the intention of subsequent use. The Bible was not preserved like that. The words of the Bible copied and recopied with the intention for future generations to read and enjoy, to learn, to use and reuse them to find God in other contexts. I have found comfort in these stories. But over time, my relationship with this book has changed—primarily because of my experience with trauma.

I have begun to see that these treasured stories were written by people like me who had experienced trauma in their time. The writers of the Bible were human like us; they asked the same kinds of questions we ask. These words and stories have been preserved with the intent that we would use them again and again to understand the meaning(s) of life. They were not creating a museum of stories; they were passing down life to us. Life as they had experienced it and life as they understood those experiences.

In the summer of 2002 I took my first summer language class, a 10-week intensive Greek course. Each day I woke, went to the gym, and then drove to class where I learned one new lesson in Greek grammar. Then I went home and learned 20 vocabulary words, practiced the grammar du jour, and translated ten sentences from Greek to English. My first seminary friend, Bridget, and I loved learning the languages. Her expertise was grammar; my expertise was vocabulary. Between the two of us we were a force to be reckoned with. But even with our abilities we could only decode about 20 verses per hour. Regardless of what we knew, we always had to consult with really big books. And after consulting with the big books, I would return to my desk and have to find my place again. Translating is a slow process. I felt as if I was crawling through the stories at the pace of a "herd of turtles walking through peanut butter." (That's one of Pete's favorite phrases.) I was slowly moving through the stories, and the slow pace allowed me to hear the stories anew. I even began to understand myself more.

When we read slowly our brains ask a lot of questions. Every word can open up an entirely new image. Every new image reveals a new question. When I began to translate the Bible from its original languages it was as if I had been reading the Bible in black and white, and then one day I got a color version. The story line is the same, the characters the same, the action the same, but nothing beats the color of the story. I loved the color version so much—I didn't care how many images or questions that it provoked...just don't send me back to black and white.

Take the story of Noah's ark. This story is so familiar that we decorate children' rooms with animals and rainbows. Well, if you're reading the story of Noah's ark really slowly because you're reading it in another language, you see the story is less about rainbows and animals and more about God destroying the world by drowning. God tells one family, Noah's family, that they will not drown if they build an ark. They do. They cut the timber and follow God's blueprints for a way out of the impending doom that faces the earth as they know it. And then God closes the door, while their neighbors still think Noah is crazy for building an ark. And then…then it begins to rain. The neighbors begin to yell "Let us in! Let us in!" But Noah and his family don't let them in. Instead, the waters rise and the people drown, all while Noah and his family are in a floating bunker with smelly, noisy animals.

How did this story become about God saving Noah's family and not about God destroying humanity? I don't want to see "Noah décor'" unless it has people drowning or screaming in the surrounding water. This story should give us nightmares; why are we decorating with it?

When we read the story in our familiar tongue, we jump past the death and destruction. We jump to the promise at the end with the rainbow. If we read it in our familiar tongue, we even think that the story ends with the rainbow. But it doesn't. When Noah gets to dry land, he gets drunk. If we read the story fast, that's just plain odd. But, in the slow-motion version of Noah, in the color version of Noah's ark, it makes complete sense. By the time we get to dry land, we're so disturbed by death that it makes complete sense that Noah got drunk. In fact, when we read it slowly, we can smell the stench of animals cooped up together— when we read it slowly we hear Noah's family bickering after having no personal space—when we read it slowly, we want to get drunk *with* Noah.

Interpretation takes time; making meaning takes time. Searching for God takes time. We can't make sense of anything, in scripture or in life, until we see the full picture, smell the surroundings, hear the sounds of all the characters. In order to do that, we've got to jump in with both feet. We can't stand on the sidelines merely cheering for God to show up.

That's what all my crying was about. For better or for worse, I had jumped into life with MS. I couldn't find the sidelines from where people seemed to be standing and offering me advice. I had come close and personal with a progressive disease. An academic or scientific understanding of what was happening to Pete was not enough. I don't think we can keep trauma at arm's length any more than I think we can interpret holy texts without tainting our understanding with our own ideas. A real search for God requires full involvement. Who we are becomes part of the question of who God is; who God is becomes part of the question of who we are.

Searching for God is almost like cooking. When we begin looking for God, the stew is simple—just a few ingredients cooked together. The flavor is suitable for a child, not too spicy, simple vegetables. But as we mature, the list of ingredients grows. The flavors become more intricate. When we experience qualifying events, life adds new learning, new experiences, new understanding. Trauma changes the flavor of the stew.

My friend, Ana, told me that before her Italian grandma passed away, the family wanted to make sure that someone knew how to make her sauce recipe. Apparently, her Italian gravy was like none other. My friend set out to learn the secret family recipe. One Sunday afternoon, while the family gathered over football, she watched intently, writing down each detail as she and grandma prepared supper. The meal was wonderful, her stomach was full, and her heart was richer knowing that this family tradition would continue with her. A few weeks later, Ana attempted the sauce herself and brought it over to grandma's house for a private tasting. The gravy was very good, but it was not grandma's gravy. There was a hint of spice that did not blend the same. Her grandmother commenced with the questions to make sure that Ana had not omitted or added anything incorrectly. She had not. The mystery continued with each attempt at the famous gravy.

One day, the grandma came to the granddaughter's house to find the cause of the defective sauce. Imagine the surprise when grandmother's sauce, made at the granddaughter's home, had the same skewed taste. How can that be? There cannot be a special flavor added simply because of the house. The grandmother was determined to figure out this riddle, and so she carried all of the needed supplies for the gravy from her house over to the granddaughter's house to try the famous sauce again. The sauce was finally a success, and when taking inventory on the differences in the sauce. The only variable was the pot. Grandma's pot made grandma's gravy. Granddaughter's pot made granddaughter's gravy.

Into my pot then...my past, my present, my understandings, my questions. Into my pot...Pete's diagnosis of MS, my tears, my confusion. Into my pot...the people around me and all of their life experiences. I give it a little stir and see what I come up with. Making stew is not an exact science. Searching for God isn't either.

God in the Bible, God in Me

Prior to seminary, I believed that the Bible was central to a person's relationship with God. Alive and rich, the words of the Bible leaped from the page in a hundred different directions and encouraged, comforted, and reconciled anyone courageous enough to listen to them. These sacred scriptures were my friends. They were reliable. My parents raised me to seek truth in the scriptures of the Christian tradition. I went to Sunday school; they sought out friends for me who shared similar religious interests, and we talked about faith at home together. The foundation of what has now become my vocation in Christian ministry rests largely on my parental upbringing. For me, faith was not only a Sunday activity. My belief in God invaded the other days of the week.

From a very early age, I memorized scripture that encouraged me to be kind, patient, and peaceable. These words of scripture really helped me in my day to day life. If life trapped me in its rat race, I remembered, "It was for freedom that Christ set us free." (Galatians 5:1) When I didn't know why I believed, I recalled the words of the psalmist that says, "Because your love is better than life, my lips will praise you." (Psalm 63:3) When I was afraid, the writer of John reminded me that Jesus said, "In this world, you will have trouble but take heart, I have overcome the world." (John 16:33). The words of the Bible were written by and about people just like me, people in need of freedom and faith, people who longed for solace and security, and they found those things in the God of heaven and earth. My needs are not new. A lot of people went before me and looked to God for help. I am not alone, I stand in a rich tradition of people who have found understanding of God in the scriptures.

My childhood exploration of these sacred words grew into a deep love of them. And, if I'm honest, I developed a radical reliance on them for joy, for peace, and for patience. Like many others, I moved from home to college and needed to reinvent my faith for the person I was becoming. I found a dear friend, Sarah, who accepted a dare with me to read the Bible for 90 days in a row. We were to touch base with each other every day for 90 days and share where we "found" God that day. This daily exercise created not a dependence on the scriptures, but a deep belief in finding meaning for my life through reading and interpreting the scriptures. Each day I set out believing that God indeed had a word of advice, comfort, and kindness for Sarah and for me. Some days we sat over dinner listening intently to the great truths that we were assimilating into our bucket of knowledge. Other days we caught the last five minutes of the day together, sitting in the dorm lobby whispering that we weren't sure what God said, but we "think" it might be this or that. As I remember it, we made the 90 days, but the ground rules insisted that if one of us were to miss a day, we both had to start over. We simply did not entertain the notion of starting over. The 90 days ended, and we were forever changed. I believed that God wanted to be found, and specifically, I believed that God could be found through the sacred writings of the Bible.

While my daily search for God in my undergraduate days seemed simplistic, the principles still remain part of my search for God today. I believe God wants to be revealed. I also believe we must stop long enough to recognize or experience what or how God is being revealed in and around us. And often, the comings and goings of God, the work of God, are seen and experienced through human activity. We are the hands and feet of God. We offer the words of encouragement to one another. God intermingles in the comings and goings of our human lives. But my search for God still is rooted very much in these words passed down to us in the stories of the Bible.

My formal study of God in seminary turned my search for understanding God into a wrestling match of sorts. I was invited to question and search for God and about God in new ways, with new books and new ideas. I could pin an old understanding to the mat of my studies. I could take down a belief that no longer served me or seemed no longer viable. I wrestled with what I saw, what I knew, and what I believed.

The Hebrew Scriptures tell a story of the ancestor Jacob who wrestled with a man. We don't know who this man is, but the experience of wrestling with him changed Jacob forever. He even got a new name out of the deal—from this point onward in the story, Jacob would be called Israel. But his new life, the life after his qualifying event, carried a price: Jacob left the wrestling mat with a limp.

Before the wrestling match, Jacob's life was messy. He had stolen his brother's birthright early in life. He ran away and fell in love. His father-in-law-to-be made him work for seven years in order to marry. But then his father-in-law tricked him and switched brides on his wedding night. Jacob had to work another seven years for the bride he wanted. Once Jacob had those two wives, they competed for his affection via how many children they bore for him. In an effort to win this competition, they each pushed Jacob to bear children with their maidservants. I wonder how Jacob dealt with his trauma? I wonder how Jacob searched for God? I wonder if and when Jacob found God in his life, the confusing, the hurtful, the decisions, the trauma?

You see, I was reading with the assumption that God wanted to be involved in every aspect of Jacob's life. I believed God wanted to be involved in every aspect of my life—a failed driver's test, a broken heart, a college rejection letter, a damaged relationship. I was always asking, wrestling even with the question "Where is God in this?" I believed that God was present, I only needed to look, to reflect, to keep wrestling. At the end of Jacob's fight, when it seemed Jacob might prevail, the man began to retreat. But Jacob grabbed hold of the man and demanded that he give Jacob a blessing.

The wrestling man gave Jacob both a new name and a blessing. But he got one more thing…a limp. As a last move, the man reached in and wrenched Jacob's hip causing him to limp. I rarely think of the patriarch Jacob as walking with a limp as he led the tribes of Israel. Yet with each step he took he was reminded that wrestling for meaning and understanding comes with a cost.

Whether we are wrestling with meaning through the

scriptures we love, or wrestling with trauma that we've experienced, wrestling comes with a cost. When we jump into these life experiences searching for meaning, understanding, or the presence of God, we come away with a very different perspective of the world around us. And more importantly, we understand ourselves to have changed. Two years into this diagnosis, two years as a pastor, two years of listening to questions and looking for answers, I was ready to demand a blessing, and before I fully got it, I had begun to limp.

ARTICLES PEOPLE GIVE ME

ABOUT THREE YEARS AFTER PETE'S DIAGNOSIS, a very good friend and colleague dropped an article on my desk that began with the statistic "72% of marriages dealing with chronic illness end in divorce." The statistic was in a larger font than the rest of the article. I gulped the sentence down in one bite, put the article down, and never read the rest of it. Married people who are struggling with a chronic illness don't need an article to tell them that marriages suffer. They may, however, need someone to keep the sharp objects out of reach.

Another well-meaning person gave both Pete and I several articles about alternative medicine and holistic approaches to healing as it pertained to MS. Well- meaning—of course. One of my favorite ways Pete would handle this kind of "care" was to come home and say to me, "Everyone knows someone with MS and everyone has a treatment that no one has heard of—if only I would take this plant and rub it into my belly button! Presto—no more MS."

Within the next month my dad gave me an article entitled "Resilient People." Out of sheer rebellion left over from adolescence, I stuck the article in my briefcase and never read it. From time to time, my dad would quote the article in conversation, saying things like, "Well, Beth, it's like the article said, 'resilient people take care of themselves. They eat right, exercise, or take time for themselves.'" I couldn't help but feel people were trying to fix me and my feelings by reminding me of all the right things I should do, but in reality they were making themselves feel better about being with me. People were deeply uncomfortable with my being emotional. When I would cry (because crying was and always is a reasonable response), I would watch people—family—get uncomfortable with me. Some would muster enough strength to ask if I had a therapist. The answer: Yes, of course I did.

I was spending more energy and time taking care of myself than I ever had. We ate slow-cooked, local, fresh food. I baked my own bread. Because I enjoyed cooking, I took time to do so regularly. I journaled. I slept well. I exercised fairly regularly. I went to a weekly yoga class. I was going to therapy, with and without Pete. Of all my healing choices, the most effective was time with my dear friends; we call ourselves the "sistas." My sistas lingered with me, listened to me, cried with me. I remember one perfect afternoon when they played with me. They purchased tickets to Lilith Fair. They made sure to pick me up so that I didn't have to drive myself. They knew I was doing all I could to take care of me. Sometimes they took their turn offering me care.

Of course, I know these articles about the divorce rate, the need for self-care, and even the holistic treatments were all well-meaning. These folks loved me. Taking time to give me an article that made them think of me was really touching. It reminded me that I am not alone. I had so many people who desperately wanted me to find a way to move through life with more light and grace. Taking care of my marriage and myself were, and are, important to experiencing light and grace. Eating well, taking supplements, and being open to alternative treatment is important. But that said, Pete and I had a solid marriage. We not only loved each other. We liked each other. We enjoyed being together. We enjoyed talking and having coffee. We enjoyed watching movies. We enjoyed our home and our family. When illness struck, life changed. Some of these articles seemed to be begging us to hold on to what we had, before MS hit. Holding on to what we had was moving against the tide. Instead of finding a way to hold on, we needed to give ourselves permission to change and grow with the changes. We needed to be forgiving and gracious to ourselves and one another as we adjusted to our new normal.

Once we went to a little sandwich dive that we had been talking about, but we forgot to discuss whether it was accessible for him. I was aware that people were staring at him as he went through the door with his walker. I was aware that people glanced at me, too. Everywhere we went it was a production. And this may seem like a small thing, but Pete could no longer open the door for me. I don't *need* the door opened for me. But it was no longer an option. How was I to care for myself regarding that? How would I adapt to that reality in a healthy way?

While I was trying to adapt and change, and trying to take care of myself, it became unquestionably clear that forever when people asked me how I was doing, I answered by telling them how Pete was doing. And most people didn't even notice that I hadn't answered the question. I think it's because most people actually wanted to know more about Pete than about me. There was one person who mentioned it; she was also a caregiver to her spouse who suffered with a form of dementia. She said, "Isn't it interesting that in answer to how are you, we talk about how our spouse is doing?" We both agreed, however, that how our spouses were doing was intertwined with how we were doing.

If Pete had a bad day, my agenda changed. If he had a good week, I had a lot more freedom. But this woman and I both believe that only answering how our spouses were doing was somehow withholding information. We were not divulging information about ourselves. We were sparing the person on the other end of the question the details of how difficult or painful our experience had become. We were allowing ourselves to become invisible, swallowed up by what was happening to our partners. If I focused all of my attention on Pete and his illness, then I could ignore myself and no one would have to be uncomfortable with what was happening to me.

Maybe I needed the articles more than I thought. Maybe we all need reminders to care for ourselves, to take ourselves seriously, to make our own health a priority. I was deeply grateful to have people in my life who believed that taking care of my marriage and taking care of myself was important. It is certainly true that resilient people care for themselves, and 72% of marriages dealing with a chronic illness end in divorce. Alternative treatment and nutritional supplements are gifts from above. It's also true that chronic illnesses suck, and we are forever changing from the losses that we are experiencing.

LOSS

ONE DAY PETE BROKE A MUG as he was putting away the dishes. I wasn't bothered by Pete breaking a mug; I was glad that it wasn't another wine glass (I was down to three reasonably sized wine glasses). But that morning I had woke thinking about the friend who had given me that particular mug. The mug read, "Friends are forever," and it had a cat on it. Not quite my style but when I drank coffee from it, I remembered this friend. And the honest truth was something had changed in this friendship. I feared the changes had to do with Pete's illness and the many changes his illness had created in our daily lives.

Warning: I tend to make bigger meaning out of little losses.

Years ago my youngest son Joe's cat died. It was the year he went off to college. Pete found the cat looking sick, and when he tried to get up, the cat convulsed and then flopped down dead. It was quite dramatic. Pete did the dreaded duty of telling Joe that his cat had died. Joe came home, grieved for his childhood pet, offered some love to the other cat that was still alive, and then I did the clean-up duty of taking my son and his dead cat to the vet for its "burial."

I remember telling a friend this story. I said something like "One of Joe's cats died. There were two cats—brothers—and the one who died was outgoing and fun-loving. The one who is still alive is melancholy and quiet. Since Joe has been at college, he's lost some of his fun-loving ways around me. I can't stand that he is changing and that I may be losing part of my little boy." My friend interrupted me and said, "Sometimes cats just die, Beth. There doesn't have to be a bigger meaning to it!" I honestly looked at her stunned, "What?!" Of course, there was larger meaning!

Little things happen, and they connect to bigger events, people, things, and memories. They conjure joy, love, kindness, sadness, loss, rejection, desire, hope. I needed the little things to help me understand the big things. I needed to pick up the broken pieces of a mug on the kitchen floor because the broken pieces would help me understand that when trauma strikes, friendships change. When I get hit by external sources, the way I go through life changes. When we change, our friendships change... sometimes they withstand those changes and sometimes they break.

I pick up one large piece still intact from the fall; I realize that it can still hold quite a bit of something; maybe not liquid, but it makes me imagine how our friendship can change. It can become something different. When I search for the little shards of pottery that shot far away from the mug, I wonder what pieces of me, of Pete, of my friendships, have simply shattered? I allow this broken mug to help me explore the inner landscape of this trauma we are living through. Pieces of us had shattered. Little bits of us were still undiscovered.

The mug was teaching me things, helping me understand myself. What if, like the mug, I couldn't hold "stuff" like I always had? What if others would need to hold "stuff" for me? Will others help Pete and me when we can't help ourselves? You see, I wasn't a mug, and when I break or shatter from falling, I wasn't going to get tossed into the trash. I was having to live with my brokenness. Pete was having to live with his brokenness. We had cracks and scars. Sometimes we stumbled on pieces that we thought we had lost. We glued ourselves back together as best as we could.

Or maybe sometimes mugs break, and I should stop looking for a deeper meaning.

HEALING POWER OF PASTA

THE AFTERNOON AFTER WE FOUND OUT THAT PETE had MS I was setting up a luncheon at church with one of the members of my congregation, a physician, Lori. Before I knew it, I blurted it out: "They found nonspecific white matter on Pete's MRI. They say he has MS." Then I realized that I had just told her something that we weren't ready to tell anyone. "I'm so sorry. I shouldn't have told you. I can't really ask you not to tell anyone, but please don't tell anyone just yet." She, as a physician, was comfortable with confidentiality. She keeps secrets all the time. Nonetheless, I apologized for what to me seemed like crossing a line as her pastor. She should not be keeping my secrets; I should be keeping hers.

We all need our secrets kept. Pastors are no different. We need people in our lives who are comfortable knowing about our brokenness. We need people who are not afraid to struggle alongside us. One of the things we learned was not every friend stays around after trauma. But some did. In the beginning of learning of Pete's diagnosis with MS, we were so fragile and unaware, shocked, and disoriented. We had two friends who held our secrets and handled us with care.

Every Sunday, for nearly a year, I finished up at church, got home, changed clothes, and headed to the house of our friends, John and Linda. Linda made homemade Italian gravy almost each week. We feasted on pasta and her gravy and finished off plenty of wine. These Sunday night meals, filled with drinking and eating and laughing, will go down in my memory as some of the best meals I've ever had.

Our lives, and our secrets, lived at that dinner table. And one of the great things about girlfriends is that we want the "play by play." When we tell a story, we want to know all of the details. Sunday night was when I got to tell my story with all the details—the doctor's visits, the research, the questions, the hurt, the joy, and everything in between.

When they asked, "How are you?" they wanted to know the answer. And they asked every week. I knew we were repeating ourselves. But they didn't care. If they did, they never let on. We filled our plates with pasta, and we gorged on the feast of real friendship.

TEAM SCIBIENSKI

WHEN PETE'S MS WAS FIRST DIAGNOSED, our son's girlfriend (now wife), Faith, suggested that we register for an MS walk together. She said, "We'll have our own Team Scibienski." The sentiment was loving, and her intention was to come closer to me in my grief, but all I heard was that we needed a "Team Scibienski." And at the time, I didn't want to need a Team Scibienski. And are we going to need a whole team? How much help will we need? I tried to get excited about walking in an MS walk. I tried to imagine us gathering friends and printing t-shirts. But the honest truth was I was not ready for Team Scibienski.

For so many, jumping into friendship with people who share their particular disease or illness provides a safe place for the emotional roller coaster they are on. For so many, rushing into the fight for a cure gives purpose to an otherwise confusing journey. But Pete and me, we couldn't do it. Quite frankly, we didn't want to be with people who had MS. We had plenty of MS in our life. I knew others feel the same. In fact, the leader of the first MS support group we attended blurted out "I hate being with people with MS." He was the leader...and we understood completely.

It took us a long time to absorb the blow of the diagnosis. We couldn't do research without an onslaught of tears. At some point our youngest son, Joe, said to Pete, "Dad, why aren't you reading everything you can get your hands on? When we were younger, if we had a question, we looked it up. We read books. We went to the library. Why aren't you doing that?" Good question. The answer: We had experienced trauma and were in the grips of grief. But we didn't understand any of this.

The life we imagined had been attacked by Pete's own nervous system. Every time I tried to learn more about the disease, I became overwhelmed and confused. MS is a very individual disease. It was enough for me to do my part of the team. And my brain was at capacity trying to adjusting to the expanding scope of his needs. But Joe was right in that I was reaching my limit of knowledge, ability, compassion, or stamina. I could no longer provide for Pete in the manner I had in the past. We needed a team. The first time I felt the relief of Team Scibienski was after we had finally compiled a team of physicians we trusted to help us through this.

We began this journey with an internist. We trusted her from the start. She was calculated in her responses. She was accessible, in her hours and in her demeanor. We would see two neurologists before we settled on the third. In the beginning of this journey a physician friend, Audra said "Keep going to doctors until you believe one. Then you'll know you've found the right one for you."

This was helpful advice for us. Since MS is unique to each person, we kept digging for other options. When we first met with the third neurologist, she made it clear to me that I was not the highest octane in the room. She was in charge; she understood what was happening.

In the three years it took us to find the third neurologist, we had learned a lot about ourselves. We had lived with changes in Pete's body and had practiced finding the right words to describe those changes. During those three years we prayed and cried and yelled a lot about all those changes. We vacillated between believing his diagnosis and not believing his diagnosis. Like I said before, we still hadn't found a doctor we believed. Here is how I knew we found the one for us. At the end of our first visit, she asked if we had any additional questions. In fact, I did. I had a list of them in my journal. I began going through my list:

What if this was a back problem, not a neurological problem since I really only see the issue on his right side?

What if this is a leftover symptom from the Asiatic flu—after all, he had that when he was a kid?

And what about this...am I right in understanding that some people have nonspecific white matter on their brain and on their spinal cord but they don't have MS? Then how can we be sure this is MS?

46 BETH SCIBIENSKI

And one more thing…a friend of mine said I should ask you if it could be Lyme's Dis…"

She cut me off before I could finish the word disease. "Let me begin by saying "it is most definitely not Lyme's disease." And then her answer got a bit louder and faster, ending with "while you see primary symptoms in his leg, I see them in his hands and in his posture and with his left side as well as his right side."

She paused. She must have realized I was stunned to silence.

She took a deep breath and lowered her voice. She looked directly at Pete and said, "You have multiple sclerosis."

And then she looked at me. And nodded. Tears had begun to develop in my eyes but she did not look away. She was both strong and compassionate. I found my breath and looked right back into her eyes and I said, "Thank you."

I learned a very important lesson about myself that day. I learned that each of us on Team Scibienski have our area of expertise. My expertise was being his partner. I needed someone else to manage Team Scibienski. And we had found our leader!

It may have been the first time I exhaled since those first steps outside the Bonnie Raitt concert. We still needed a cardiologist to distinguish some confusion and treat some vascular disease outside of the neurological disease. Along the way, we collected a urologist, a pulmonologist, a therapist. We knew we would continue to add players when needed.

We hung out with these players a lot in the beginning. One visit often led to another visit and then potentially to another. They worked together, and the best advice we ever got was "Always give them a list of other physicians with whom you would like them to copy their office notes." It's easy, and they understand that working together is best for Team Scibienski.

In addition to the physician players on our team, there was me. Sometimes I felt like the coach, sometimes the overused pitcher, and sometimes I was running all over the field. It was in those times though...the times when I was clearly playing too many positions—that I remember that initial offer to form Team Scibienski. Faith meant it for more than walking an MS walk together. She wanted to suit up. She wanted a position on the team. She was saying "put me in, Coach. I want to play."

Over time, I let others in the game. One winter morning after a snowstorm, I was stressed about getting Pete safely into the car for a doctor's appointment. I had a list of things I needed to do before I could come home to pick Pete up for the appointment. and I couldn't figure out when I would shovel. My brother David called for something. and I started to cry. He came over while I was out and shoveled every last tablespoon of snow away. As I learned to ask for help, I learned that lots of people wanted to be on Team Scibienski. Mostly notably—the members of my church family.

A Table of Others

My earliest memory of church is a children's Sunday school class. I remember sitting at a table with a handful of others. There was a window nearby and what appeared to be fall sunlight coming into the room. We were doing an activity at the table and we were were talking to one another. The raw ingredients of the memory are a table, conversation, and "others."

As a pastor, as a mother, as a friend, as a colleague, as a wife, I have spent my career trying to reproduce that memory. I have tried to reproduce moments when people gather around a table to talk with "others." Generally speaking, our culture does well to draw us together with people who are similar. But being in relationship with others, those with whom you would not naturally gather, is something different. Choosing community with people who are different or with people that I do not know well takes energy and planning.

Church for me is an act of gathering with people who have a similar faith but in many other ways are quite different from me— different ages, genders, interests, abilities, and needs. Both Pete and I value this kind of community. We believe it changes us for the better. It broadens our understanding and challenges our worldview. But as we were grieving and adjusting our life to the reality of Pete's diagnosis, we reconsidered whether or not we needed to be around such a "table," or in a group with others who were experiencing the same things. We wished we knew others who could offer us support from the "inside" of the disease. We decided to look for a support group in our area.

Our first attempt at a support group went horribly. We drove to a nearby public library; we were nervous, scared, and generally stressed out. When we arrived, the people at the front desk didn't know what we were talking about. We explained that we had found the information online. We were tossed from person to person until someone finally said, "Oh yes, I know the group. They're not meeting this month." We made our way back to the car, packed the walker, and when I settled in the driver's seat, the anxiety from the build-up and the disappointment ran through me and I began to sob. This kind of crying, we decided, would only subside with fried food or cheesecake. We opted for both and headed to a diner.

I wanted a support group. (Pete probably needed one but had not actually asked for one himself.) We tried the same group again. This time Pete called first and found that they were not having a traditional meeting the next month because of the holidays. We were welcome to join them but perhaps starting the following month would be a better idea.

So, we tried again. This time, for some reason, the group had been assigned a different room than their usual one. This new room was not conducive for people with wheelchairs and scooters. The "leaders" of the group were visibly flustered by the change of environment. The air was buzzing with that frustration. Then add my own anxiety level; we weren't off to a good start.

We had been told that this group was for both those with the disease and their caregivers but I was the only caregiver in the room. Now, if you're a caregiver and you're in a room filled with folks who need help...forget that. If you're human and you're in a room with a bunch of people who clearly need help, you help. And so I helped. I helped folks find a place at the table. I helped folks get around the room. I poured soda. When we got in the car, I held back my tears. We did not go to the diner for fried food and cheesecake. We just went home and went to bed.

We tried another support group; it was at a Presbyterian church. I thought I'd feel more at home in the environment, which I did. But I still was the only support person present. This support group wasn't a "sit around a table and check in with each other" kind. Instead, there was a speaker and a time for Q&A. Pete really enjoyed this support group. Turns out he was more comfortable with information-driven groups, whereas I was still thinking I needed more relational connections. Some had suggested that I try a general "caregiver" support group. I looked into them and found the demographics of the groups didn't resemble my experience at all. Many times general caregiver groups are filled with two types of caregivers: those caring for their parents and those caring for a spouse with dementia.

At this point in my search I began to wonder whether I was looking for connection when I actually already had it. One afternoon I had lunch with three women from my church. One of the women had just moved her husband into a longterm care facility. He had severe dementia. Another woman at the table had recently found a second love in her life after having lost her husband to cancer many years earlier. The fourth seat at the table was taken by a woman my age with two teenage sons. We settled into a corner table, surrounded by windows that let in the sunshine.

A table of "others"—we brought our perspectives, our hopes, our losses, our sadness, and our longing for connection. These people in my life made me a better person. They made me think. They looked at me when I was talking, and their eyes said "I am happy to share life with you."

For the time being, I was going to stop looking for a support group of caregivers for spouses with MS. I would instead be grateful for the community of others that I already had who sat with me around a table by a window that let the sunshine in.

Falling Down
Used to be Funny

In my understanding, there seems to be two kinds of humor. The first is physical humor—hitting someone on the head, running into a wall, or falling down. The second, sarcasm. One summer, many years earlier, I was working at a youth camp where they were putting out their best sarcastic humor, and the kids just weren't laughing. We sat in team meetings simply not knowing what was wrong. The kids just didn't seem to get the jokes. So we decided to change our tactic and leave the sarcasm behind and replace it with slapstick—run into one another, throw a fish across the stage, make funny faces. It worked! The kids howled with laughter.

Running into a wall and falling down makes us laugh. In the early years of his diagnosis, Pete fell a lot. Once I knew his falling was related to MS, I wondered about our laughter response. For starters, I think we must relate to falling down in a visceral way. I also think we feel embarrassed for the one who fell. I think we feel awkward for feeling embarrassed and for the stumbling nature of humanity. We often don't know what to say or do when someone falls so there is silence. To escape the embarrassment, the awkwardness, and the horrible silence, we laugh.

Pete would often say, "I'm getting so good at falling." In reality, he fell because his nervous system had a failure of communication. He explained falling like this "it's as if I'm a cartoon figure. In one frame, I have two legs and in the next, one of my legs is erased."

One night we were on our way into John and Linda's home for her granddaughter's birthday party. I dropped Pete off at the curb to park the car. Using a walker, he began the ascent on the sidewalk to the front steps. Two or three men were out front talking and smoking cigarettes. They offered to help Pete up the steps. As a way of saying "yes," Pete pushed his walker to one of them so they could place it on the top step. But Pete wasn't close enough to the railing and he began to lose his balance. He leaned and reached for the railing. But only the top half of his body got the signal while his lower half stood still. He went down straight as a board.

I described Pete's nervous system as "sticky." His brain's instructions to his legs traveled through what seemed to be Elmer's glue. In addition to his legs not getting the message, his hands didn't get the message to reach out and break his fall. He landed on his face on a cement step. He rolled to the right...elbow, shoulder, hip, butt. Everyone watched it in slow motion. There was no laughter. So Pete told a joke; he said "well, let's see if we've got blood."

I was not laughing. No, when I spoke, I used the F-word in as many ways humanly possible. And then when I realized we were at a child's birthday party, I felt a wave of shame for using the F-word. As the news of Pete's fall made its way inside, the birthday girl came out to greet us and said, "I had a bloody nose once; it hurt." Then she added, "You need to put peroxide on it. But that will burn. I don't like peroxide. If it burns, that's how you know there's a cut there." Then she started over, "I had a bloody nose once; it hurt..."

While the rest of the party went uninterrupted, the birthday girl stayed with us in the bathroom while we used up a box of tissues to find out what was bleeding. When no one else knew what to say, she didn't have a problem filling the silence. She connected with us easily. When Pete's cuts were all bandaged up, she took us by the hand and asked if we would play Parcheesi with her.

I don't remember the last time I played Parcheesi. Certainly, I wasn't married yet. I wasn't a mom yet. I wasn't a caregiver yet. I also think the last time I played Parcheesi, I didn't think that falling down was funny. When I was a young, Parcheesi-playing human, I bet I was more like this little girl who knew that falling down hurts and if there is a cut, peroxide is going to hurt too. Falling down hurts. And that awkward feeling—it's empathy followed by fear followed by vulnerability. And when the night was finished, I was grateful for tissues, for peroxide, and for little girls who are way more comfortable with the human condition than I was.

Meltdowns

WITH THE OPTION OF FALLING DOWN LURKING around every corner, stress was my way of life. People who are caregivers and people who are chronically ill are stressed individuals. We were living each day acutely aware that we were not in control of our lives. We no longer believed any of us were in control. The land underneath us, our foundation, seemed to be melting. Stress led to the secondary emotion, anger. We didn't look angry on the outside but we—okay, I can only speak for me—I was angry all the time. I suppressed it as best as I could. And then my anger turned inward, becoming depression. I believed the world around me expected me to be kind and merciful and compassionate, and I wasn't any of those things. So in addition to being stressed, angry, and depressed, I was ashamed of myself.

Everyone has limits to their amount of compassion. But I reached mine so regularly in those first few years. I came face to face with my limitations so often, I wasn't just ashamed. I was afraid I was really a horrible person. My limitations, my finiteness, frightened me. The world was unsafe and turbulent and grotesque, and I really didn't have the ability to deal with it. I lost my cool so often.

One time in an outburst of stress, resentment, confusion, and grief, I emptied most of my closet and part of Pete's closet onto the floor of our bedroom. Here's what happened: I had an event for work, and Pete was going to attend with me. I was running late from another meeting. I called on my way saying that I would need to change clothes quickly, and we would need to head out as soon as possible. He greeted me in the kitchen wearing blue dress pants that were two sizes too big and a traditional Ghanaian black and turquoise shirt. I had suggested the shirt but I assumed he would wear it with a pair of black Dockers. He looked ridiculous. We couldn't go out like that.

I ran up the steps, dressed, applied makeup as quickly as I could. Then I had to figure out what else Pete could wear. I opened his closet wondering to myself, "When did he lose so much weight?" I tore into the hangers but couldn't find black pants. I piled every pair of pants we both owned—just in case his pants had found their way into my closet somehow—onto the floor of our bedroom. I lost it. Yelling to myself essentially, "You've got to be kidding me. Where the hell are his pants? What? He only has one pair of pants that fit him? This is crazy. I don't want to shop for men's clothing. This is not my job. I can't win here...if I don't help him, he won't go with me. But I want him to go with me, so I have to help him. Why am I helping him dress himself? When did his mother stop doing this? It must have been a long time ago. When did I start doing this? It must have been a long time ago."

I somehow got my inner voices to pause long enough for me to realize that I was not going to find the black pants. So I chose a different shirt to match the oversized pants and we finally got in the car and headed out.

Once in the car, however, my inner monologue wanted me to say something to Pete rather than stew about it silently. My mind was at war with itself, honestly. These were not audible voices but without question, I was of two minds.

One: Talk to him. Tell him how you're feeling.

Two: Don't do it. It won't make it any better. This is your life now. Deal with it.

One: But you're not his mother. You should not have to help him dress!

Two: Let it go. No matter what your expectations, realistic or reasonable, gone are the days when you will get what you want.

One: Oh, for crying out loud, just use your words. Talk to him.

Voice number One won. Voice number one was angry and agitated. Voice number one began ramping up the volume, because talking is always better and talking loudly is the best.

And so I began to speak loudly, arguing with Pete about the injustice of having to help someone with tasks that they can do themselves...like pick out clothes. I yelled the entire car ride. By the time we had arrived at the event, voice number two was mostly tapping her foot and shaking her head at me. She knew talking about it would leave me feeling foolish. I had spent the car ride yelling at a chronically ill person, and now I was to walk into the event, a calm, collected, nonanxious pastor.

And I don't know if it was voice number one or voice number two or hell…who cared at this point, I felt like a horrible human. I had no patience, no compassion. I was unable to control my emotions and I yelled at a sick person. I mean really…who yells at a sick person?

The answer to that question is…a lot of people. Sick people are human, and they're hurtful and they're selfish. They aren't always good at communicating what they need, and sometimes they demand more than they need. In a lot of ways sick people are no different from well people.

After this meltdown, I was a mix of embarrassed, angry, confused, bitter, helpless, vulnerable, depressed, discouraged, and disgusted. Once I got my bearings, I tried to listen to what was really wrong. What was this all about? Was it really about mismatched clothes? Was it really about having to help Pete purchase clothes that fit him? What was this reallly about?

You see, I had wanted to get dressed up and go on a date with my partner. I wanted to have a nice glass of wine and share a tasty meal together. For me it was a date and Pete showed up in clothes that didn't match. I wanted something to feel like it used to feel. But our life had already changed so much. The ground under my feet seemed to be melting out from under me. Everywhere I stepped it was slippery.

When we returned home I sloshed over to the closet and picked up the piles of clothes. I hated that the ground was melting, or that it felt like it was melting, or that I felt that I was melting down. I hated what was happening to Pete, and by extension what was happening to us and to me. I wished there had been some turnaround that night. I wished that we had made some great change in how we were going to manage the melting underneath us. Instead, I did what anyone does when their feet are slipping, I walked slower. I took small deliberate steps. I was worn out and I needed to ask for help. So I asked my sons to help with clothes shopping for their father. And then I resolved to find time for rest and play, even if it was in a melted environment.

CARING FOR THE CAREGIVER

MOST PEOPLE GO TO THE DOCTOR ONCE A YEAR. For those dealing with chronic illnesses, doctors are practically part of the family. Our doctors knew our weekly activities; they remembered our kids' names. Take for example, our chiropractors, Dr. Mike and Dr. Heidi.

I had gone to the chiropractor my whole life. Not Pete. In the second year of his diagnosis, he gave it a try. The night after his first adjustment, he slept through the night. He couldn't remember the last time that happened. Sleeping for the chronically ill is like currency. We assume with MS that a person's neurons fire multiple times in order to accomplish simple tasks, like moving the right leg. This meant that Pete's body was actually working multiple times harder than my body. His body got tired quicker. Sleep was his friend. Sleep generated more energy. Sleep helped his system reboot. I started taking Pete to the chiropractor every week. And I would treat myself to an adjustment every other week.

Sometimes I wondered whether this was necessary for me. I experienced stress for sure, but did I need my back adjusted this often? Yes. Why? This was one of the only times during my week where someone else cared for me.

Every week they looked me in the eye and asked how was *I* doing. They touched me, lovingly, as physicians and companions on life's journey. These two physicians knew a portion of my life better than anyone else. They saw me by Pete's side every week. They saw my ups and downs. They listened to my story, and they held it in trust.

One week Pete was having a particularly weak spell. He stumbled and fell as he entered the waiting room. Dr. Mike took over. He helped Pete up and started with treatment. Then he motioned for me to follow him. We headed into their coffee room. Having never been in there, I took in the sights of their personal space—nothing more than a closet really, with a coffee maker, some mugs, and a place for their stuff. I looked back at Mike and he asked me, "How are *you*?" fully expecting an honest answer from me.

I started to say "this kind of thing happens all the time. Pete gets tired. Pete falls. This has been a bad week." But Mike interrupted me and asked again, "But how are *you*?" I finally let go of the tears I had been holding back for three days. While I cried, he told me about his experiences with his dad who had Parkinson's. He used words like frustrated, disappointed, exhausted.

He asked if I was taking care of myself. There was that concern again—the people who loved me the most wanted to make sure I was taking care of myself. While I appreciated that question, I often felt judged by it. If my answer was yes, then whatever I was doing must not be working because clearly I look horrible or rundown. If my answer was no, then I felt as if I got caught not taking care of myself when clearly I know that is very important. How many times have I heard "you must put your own mask on first if you are going to be able to help someone else?"

So back to Mike. He asked me "Are you taking care of yourself?" I said, "Yes, I exercise, I do yoga, I read, I write, I cook. I have friends and... I come to the chiropractor." He smiled and waved me out of the coffee room and into a treatment room saying, "Let's get at that then."

Lying face down on the table, I judiciously allowed my tears to leak out while Mike massaged knots out of my back and straightened me out again. Having cared for me, he grabbed my hands and lifted me back into my life as a caregiver.

Breathing and Grieving

IN YOGA I LEARNED THAT I CAN START OVER with every new breath. With every breath, we can start over again and again. I practiced breathing—in and out. The more I practiced, the more I began to trust that I truly could start over whenever I wanted. Meltdowns came and went. I practiced breathing—in and out. Pete still fell some days. I practiced—in and out. Our lifestyle changed. I practiced breathing—in and out. If I closed my eyes and practiced breathing, inevitably I would open my eyes to a new moment.

With the practice of starting over I began to see MS as only part of our lives. When I practiced breathing, my inhale reminded me that we have a fabulous family. Two grown boys, Dan and Joe, each maturing and interacting with the world in a way that any parent would be proud. My exhale set that scene as the backdrop for my new moment. My inhales drew a picture of our loving daughter-in-law, Faith. She is incredibly generous with her heart and we love her. My exhale set a new scene, unimaginable without her.

When I inhaled, I saw our huge townhome and on my exhale I imagined a lovely meal that I had planned for supper. When I inhaled, I saw the farm to which we belong, and my exhale gave thanks for the earth that brings the harvest of the field. I inhaled the thought of a sip of wine and I exhaled the amazing, faithful friends I have. I inhaled the love Pete and I have for one another, and I exhaled thanks for meaningful work that I've been given.

At this point in our story, Pete had had the diagnosis of MS for five years. It was in this fifth year that we became grandparents to a little girl named Julia. In many ways, she changed my life as dramatically as MS had.

MS was only a portion of our lives and yet...it touches every breath in and every breath out. MS didn't keep to itself; it interacted with every portion of our lives. The same family that brings joy worried more about Pete these days. Our beautiful home was littered with assistive devices. Our scrumptious meals and our wine intake were altered by dietary needs. I had to balance work more thoughtfully and when we went out with friends, the where and when was now determined by levels of fatigue and handicap accessibility.

Often when I was practicing breathing in and out, when I tried to start over, I closed my eyes only to open them to the same stress just in a new moment. Pete was losing mobility. We were losing restful sleep hours. We were no longer able to go to the same places we enjoyed. We were no longer able to keep the same level of activity. We were losing who we were and we were losing who we thought we would be at this point in our life and our marriage. As much as our days were filled with life, we faced daily deaths. Folks who live with chronic illness face mini-deaths every day.

My grief button was pushed over and over again. I started to think we only have one grief button. No matter the loss, big or small, the grief button got pushed. Mine was being overused and I started to think it was malfunctioning. Any loss, big or small, resulted in an onslaught of tears. Whether I spilled milk or had to change weekend plans, my grief button was pushed. Regardless of the intensity of the loss, my grief button was responding with the full measure of grief I was suffering. The grief I was experiencing because of this trauma had created an intense mix of anxiety and depression. The trauma of Pete's diagnosis had turned our lives upside down. The chaos around me had me grieving day and night. I worried all the time. I was definitely inhaling, but perhaps not exhaling.

My friends and our family play this game regularly...it's a mixture of Pictionary and telephone. We call it the paper game. It's since been made into a boxed game that one can purchase. We write a phrase and then the person next to us draws the phrase, then the next interprets the phrase into words, then the next draws the interpretation. And down the line it goes. When the game is done, the journey of the original phrase is typically nothing short of hilarious. One time when we were playing this game, I interpreted someone's drawing as "Dad fell down the steps." After I said it, silence fell over the room and I realized that the paper game had just acted like a Rorschach test and my anxiety and grief were on display for everyone to see.

The option of falling was everywhere for me. Every time Pete walked down the steps, I held my breath. Every time he got in and out of the car, I held my breath. Every time he got in and out of bed, I held my breath. I was trying so hard to hold things together I was inhaling, holding onto the life we had as tight as I could, but I wasn't exhaling. I needed to exhale; I needed to learn to let go. I needed to realize that we could not stay in a house with steps. At some point we were going to need to move. I needed to accept that we were going to trade in his walker for a wheelchair sooner than we thought. I needed to stop experiencing mini-deaths as something I had to endure and allow myself to grieve these mini-deaths, these losses, so that we could move onto whatever life would be afterward. I needed to exhale.

CHRISTIANS BELIEVE
IN THE RESURRECTION

CHRISTIANS BELIEVE IN THE RESURRECTION. For sure it's not an easy doctrine to believe. I mean after all, when was the last time any of us saw someone rise from the dead? I remember sitting around with a few friends discussing the resurrection. We had all just lost a dear friend, Dave, to brain cancer. One of my friends asked us what we would do if Dave walked through the door? I said I would freak out—that is if I recognized him. In the Christian resurrection story, Jesus' friends didn't recognize him when he showed up after his death.

Christians believe in resurrection. We believe that death is not the end. Death is an avenue for new life. In the natural world, we see this all the time. A seed must die for a plant to grow.

I have a friend, Dawn, who served a very small church with a declining membership. They were a farming community. But instead of corn, those fields were now filled with homes. And those homes were now filled with families who commuted to work outside of the area and spent their Sundays at soccer games. In the last 20 years, this church had tried to resuscitate the life that used to be. There was even a suggestion that they resuscitate the beloved spaghetti dinners to raise enough funds to pay their bills. My friend offered what I believe was a prophetic word, "Christians don't believe in resuscitation; we believe in resurrection. And in order for something to resurrect, something must first die."

While I was a chaplain, I watched a group of doctors resuscitate an elderly gentleman. Resuscitation is a gruesome act. It often involves broken bones and blood. While physicians monitored blood pressure and breathing, I monitored grief and loss. Everyone in the room wanted to save life. I wanted death. I wasn't callous to the family or the doctor's desire to prevent death. I get that not everyone is comfortable with "do not resuscitate" orders. The doctors did not save this man. He suffered yet another major heart attack. And his last minutes on earth were traumatic.

Resuscitation is about bringing life back, about keeping death at bay. We cling to our lives—exposing our lives to traumatic acts of resuscitation just to hold onto what we know. We tried all kinds of things to resuscitate the life that we knew. If Pete took loads of Vitamin D or CoQ10 or tried a new drug, then certainly his symptoms would subside. Or if I found a hobby that could occupy my time while Pete slept most of the day, then I would be happy with my life. Or if we just tried new music in our church, then for sure loads of people would start coming through our doors. We fight death; we fight loss. We ward off death; we resuscitate. There are obviously some situations that require some more grit. Sometimes in life we need to keep working at something. But there are a lot of times when we need to stop for a second and imagine an end. Stop resuscitating. Stop. Let go. Allow death to happen. Embrace loss. Wait for resurrection.

For us, living with chronic illness was about managing losses. Pete started out using a walking stick that Joe gave him. Then he moved to a cane with a four-pronged foot. Then, he used a traditional walker. Then he got one with a seat. Then, he got an even fancier one, where the seat back could swing to the opposite side, transforming it into a transport wheelchair. (This was called a rollator.) Pete had secondary progressive multiple sclerosis. There was a trajectory and it was a downward slope. It was slow moving, but it was moving in the direction of loss. Incremental, little losses one after the other after the other.

When Pete and I could no longer do certain things or go certain places, we adjusted and sometimes those adjustments seemed bitter. I had grown to understand that bitterness was a sign that I was still trying to resuscitate. I didn't want the life we imagined to die. I wanted to try to keep it alive. I clung to the life we had. I clung to the dreams we dreamed together. But when our dream was dying, or when MS had taken Pete's ability to walk, I wanted to have the courage to say, "Do not resuscitate."

I wanted the faith needed to imagine resurrection instead of resuscitation. I wanted to be able to say, "Do not resuscitate that dream. Let it die. Wait for resurrection." O, "Do not resuscitate that plan. Let it die. Wait for resurrection."

When I was unable to let dreams or plans die, I woke up each day proverbially breaking bones and cleaning up the blood from another round of resuscitation. When clinging won over courage, I created more chaos, more loss, more yelling which left me exhausted and spent—still living with the ideas, plans, and dreams that were ready to die.

Do not resuscitate. Christians believe in resurrection.

PRAYER

SICKNESS IS PART OF THE HUMAN CONDITION. We are incredibly fragile. We bruise and bleed fairly easily. And as true as it is that we are headed toward death, along the way our bodies will heal from a lot of ailments. We break bones, and with the help an xray and a cast, we heal. We contract diseases and often with treatment, we survive. Pete had multiple sclerosis. Although we had only just found out, he probably contracted it two decades earlier. We did not know how or why.

We hate this lack of knowledge. No one wants to accept having to live with uncertainty and danger. The question "Where is God in all of this?" turns to "Did God cause this?" "What relationship does God have with sickness?" As a pastor, I enjoy that all of these questions assume the existence of God. If we still believe there is a God, then the next step for us is finding a way to interact with God. And maybe in interacting, we might come to understand some of the mystery of the human condition. Maybe. We might.

I didn't understand a lot of what was happening to me. The world of chronic illness had opened up a whole new way of seeing and being in the world. So I turned to God in prayer. Prayer is simply talking to God. I have always approached God like a friend. If I didn't understand a friend, or if I needed to understand a friend better, what would I do? I would spend more time with him or her. I would listen. I would explore. I would watch. The specifics of how I have prayed have changed over time. I have written prayers. I have sung prayers. I have practiced silence. I have walked. I have talked.

There was a season during Pete's illness, when I woke at 3 a.m. almost every morning. In monastic Christianity, 3 a.m. is one of the "hours." There are eight fixed times for prayer and meditation during the day. The first hour is during the night at 3 a.m. In fact when I finally talked to my friends about getting up at 3 a.m., they said "Welcome to the club." I was shocked; I said, "Are you seriously trying to tell me that women everywhere are up at 3 a.m. wishing that they could sleep?" Apparently, yes. I didn't know what other women did at 3 a.m., but sometimes I made a cup of chamomile mint tea and I wrote in my journal. Other times I baked bread, rummaged through cookbooks for interesting recipes, read a book, watched a movie, watered the plants, rearranged my bookshelves, washed the dishes, made vegetable stock. And sometimes I prayed.

Now maybe I couldn't sleep at 3 a.m. because I had reached the age when women can't sleep through the night. But I was pretty sure I was unable to sleep through the night because the stress was piling up. I would get up in the middle of the night to pee, and quite frankly, my brain never stopped engaging. I thought about specific problems in my job, about broader issues in the world, about the big picture of my life. A lot of times during this season of insomnia I thought about Pete. I thought about whether he was taking all of his medication. Pete hadn't yet had major cognitive issues associated with MS, but there was too much for any one person to remember. I thought about which doctor we hadn't seen or whether or not we needed to follow up with the last one we had seen. I wondered if we were getting enough nutrients in our diet. I thought about ways Pete could get around easier. I thought about removing the obstacles that we faced.

The next time I mentioned not sleeping to my girlfriends, they said "take Tylenol PM." Again, I was shocked. I have always been such a good sleeper the idea of taking a sleep aid seemed like an extreme measure. Was this really a time for an extreme measure? I really did not like to admit how bad life was for us. But honestly, I was in crisis almost all the time. When you live with a chronic illness, "episodes" happen. Around every corner was the potential for a fall or a mishap, something forgotten or something gone wrong, the need for a new doctor or a new medication, an addition to our life, or sometimes a subtraction from our life. I lived in crisis. And that's why my friends introduced me to Tylenol PM.

Now I was a lightweight, I couldn't take more than one. I also had to take it preemptively. In other words, if I took it at 3 a.m. to get back to sleep, I was too groggy in the morning. This wasn't every day. Sometimes chamomile mint tea, sometimes Tylenol PM, and sometimes prayer, sometimes all three.

In the Divine Hours, they all begin with a portion of a verse from Psalm 67, "God, come to my assistance; Lord, make haste to help me."

In those early hours, with sleep aid or not, spoken or not, I was recognizing that I needed help. Prayer, for me, was acknowledging that I had a limit and hoping that God did not. Prayer was time set apart that recognized my frailty and my need for peace or restoration or courage or wisdom. And there was a part of me that was grateful that my soul had an alarm clock of sorts that said, "God, come to my assistance; Lord, make haste to help me." This prayer bubbled up for me throughout the day. It broke my natural patterns, like sleep and many times work. This prayer came alive in me, pushing me to accept my limit and find what is beyond.

There had been plenty of mornings when I tried everything I knew including prayer to get back to sleep, and sleep still eluded me. Sometimes the stress of being a caregiver was too much for prayer, too much for chamomile tea, even too much for Tylenol PM. There were mornings when I baked and cooked until every pan was dirty and my apron had remnants of a fitful night. There were mornings, particularly in the winter, when I saw the last bit of night and the first light of dawn. There were nights when I was so angry that I couldn't sleep and so tired that I couldn't think straight to pray.

The more I prayed about the ways I needed help, the more I began to realize how completely in over my head I was... *I can't really take care of someone who is chronically ill. This entire situation is beyond my scope, abilities and time. I will never have all of the answers or be able to remove all of the obstacles in front of Pete. I must learn to say goodbye to lots of parts of life because I can't stop loss from happening. God, come to my assistance; Lord, make haste to help me.*

There wasn't an easy fix, a magic pill, a super food to heal

MS...or heal my heart...or make my dreams come true... It was in speaking these truths that I kept coming to the need to let go. As I spoke these truths specifically to God in prayer, I faced the call to stop clinging. Prayer was not changing Pete. Prayer was not changing MS. Prayer was not changing God. Prayer was changing me. *God, come to my assistance; Lord, make haste to help me.*

SOFT EYES

MY SISTER, KRISTIN, BOUGHT ME MY FIRST YOGA MAT, a birthday gift during my last year of seminary. I started to practice with a video tape. Yes, a *video tape*. For 20 minutes, I stretched and breathed. I held strong poses, with my arms lifted to the heavens. About halfway through one of the routines, the instructor said, "Now, with soft eyes, look up."

Soft eyes make room for the peripheral. Soft eyes wonder where the end of one thing meets the beginning of another. Soft eyes help us to let go of a hard, certain glare on the world.

The *soft eyes* is called a *drishti*, a Sanskrit word that means "vision, insight or point of view." It's a gazing technique that helps with concentration while also offering a clear view of the larger picture at hand.

I hadn't been a pastor for long when Pete was diagnosed with multiple sclerosis. After three years had gone by, I realized that the stories of his illness and our losses were braided together with experiences of illness and loss within our community of faith. The personal insights that I had gained were wedded to the insights that had come from the relationships I had developed with people in our congregation. I had come to understand that Christianity was best understood and practiced as a team sport—within a community. I had learned more of God and grown more as a faithful individual because of the community around me.

I was taught that Christianity was a personal faith. I experienced Christianity through the lens and with the backdrop of the individualistic culture of America where sometimes faith is considered not only personal but private. God and I were in this together. God and I were working out my life, my goals, my needs, my wants. After all, I had accepted God into *my* heart. I prayed for others; I prayed for issues in the world. But if I am honest, the purpose of those prayers was typically because "those issues" were affecting me somehow. This side of MS, I just wasn't able to practice Christianity that way anymore. I couldn't because even with God, I couldn't do life by myself anymore. I needed others to help. It wasn't enough to be me and God against the world. And it wasn't enough to only be concerned about things that concerned me. It wasn't enough anymore because there were people in my life who cared deeply for me and Pete. There were people who sacrificed regularly for Pete and me. It was their faithful Christian witness that taught me that Christianity was a team sport.

It was a luxury, I suppose, to try and go it alone. Going it "alone" requires a lot of resources. But even if I had the large amount of resources, I no longer wanted to go it alone. I firmly understood now—we need one another.

Since Pete's diagnosis, there had been too many days when I came to God in prayer seeking guidance and understanding, hope, and healing, and when I looked up from my personal prayer, there were others in my peripheral vision who were answers to my prayers. These others were the ones who provided guidance, understanding, hope and healing. Our community of faith had embodied living answers to so many of our prayers.

When I look back on my journey in faith, whether sitting at a table with other children in Sunday school or with friends who had hugged, listened, cared for me as I was adjusting to my life as a caregiver, my faith had always been sustained through my connection with others. And connection doesn't just happen, right? I mean, my parents had to take me to church when I was a child. As an adult, I had to reach out for help. More often than now, I had to make the first move, say the first word so that those around me would know what was on my mind and in my heart. These connections, these relationships, provided grounding for me as I experienced life through the lens of chronic illness and grief. When the answers to my prayers were elusive there were others who had experience with elusive answers. When I was broken, someone else was right there beside me who had known, and sometimes still knew, brokenness. Through my *drishti*, through my soft eyes, I began to see grace. Grace for this moment, for this prayer, for this hope, for this day. These others by my side were grace in action. God was present through this grace in action. Through people in my life, God was embracing my mess, my brokenness, my fear. All along, God had been with me as I wondered, questioned, reconsidered myself, the world, and even the nature of God. When I looked up with soft eyes, my life was filled with people, with grace, with God.

REMEMBERING

IN 1994, PETE HAD DOUBLE BYPASS SURGERY. I married him in 1995. He was 18 years older than me, which means I was born the year he graduated from high school. When our relationship was getting serious, people would politely ask us if this was a "good idea." Is loving Pete a good idea? Is becoming a stepmother to two amazing young men a good idea? Was potentially becoming a young widow a good idea? Or was the question really "Did I know what I was getting into?" To that question, the answer was "No." No one knows what they're getting into with marriage. No one knows what life is going to bring.

I officiated a wedding once—a young couple from my church. They'd been together since high school. As I got to know them it was clear that they knew each other well and I wondered if I were to ask them "Do you know what you're getting yourself into?" they may actually have said, "Well...not really. I mean, life is fragile and unpredictable. But we are going to make these promises anyway." They were aware and mature beyond their physical years. And I was encouraged. Truly encouraged. I was at a phase when the vows I had taken went way beyond what I would ever have known could happen. I didn't want to project my situation onto their newly formed union, but I couldn't help but be a little fearful for them. What if the horrible happens for them, too, and what if they are left with these promises? I supposed their promises would hold strong like ours. That's what I wanted for them.

When I asked them to choose their wedding vows and the wording for exchanging their rings, they wanted them to sound like normal, everyday speech. They wanted to say something that sounded like they would actually say this in real life. We worked out a new wording for the exchange of rings that I just loved.

I give you this ring
in hope that whenever you see it
you will remember that I love you.

Again, this small act of choosing words that sounded like them was a testament to them possibly knowing something about what they were getting into. Pete and I took a stab at choosing our own words at our wedding. We reworked the famous prayer attributed to St. Francis for our wedding vows.

Pete, I vow to be an instrument of peace in your life.
Where hatred grows, I will sow love.
When I am wronged, I will open my arms in forgiveness.
When there is discord, I will bring harmony.
Where there is error, I will seek the truth with you.
When you doubt yourself, I will have faith in you...

Granted, I'm comparing the wording of their exchange of rings to my vows, but I'm so intrigued that our vows are filled with "doing"— sowing love, opening my arms, bringing harmony, seeking truth...we imagined a very busy life. I have to wonder if we believed that by doing all of those things, life would work out. If I sowed love, if I opened my arms...our life and love would be faithful, successful, meaningful, and healthy.

Four years after Pete was diagnosed, a good friend Jeff sent me a book of poems by the U.S. Poet Laureate Donald Hall. The poems were written to and for his wife Jane Kenyon, who died of cancer. When I began to read the book, I couldn't get past page 13,[1] on which he articulated how he wanted desperately to "do" something for her. Inside himself, he said there was "some four-year-old" who thought for sure if he was "thoughtful, considerate...perfect, she would not leave him." We want to do something. We want to be able to fix things when they get broken.

As he writes, he realizes not only his need or want to "do" something but that his wife had to endure the pain of others who wanted to be able to "do something" that would make her life better. He wished to care for her in some way so as to control

---

[1] Hall, Donald, *Without,* Mariner Books, 1999. page 13,

some of the chaos they were experiencing. They were both suffering. Both grieving. Both clinging to life.

I understood the question "Can I do something for you?" I, too, wanted to do something. I wanted to do something for Pete that would make life more manageable, less hurtful. I would've even settled for feeling what he was feeling, to experience some of life as he was experiencing it. For me, marriage was about participating in life together. But sometimes there was nothing to be done. Sometimes marriage was about witnessing. Witnessing to what was happening, witnessing to what was. It was this participation, this witnessing that gave feet to our vows during this time. Pete picked me; I picked him. We had a day when we made vows, grandiose as they were. We had a day when he put a ring on my finger with hopes that when I see it, I would remember that he loved me. He wanted me to remember. I wanted him to remember.

After I pronounced the young couple married, they kissed. One little kiss. Then they looked at each other, two kisses, three kisses, stop to look again. Four kisses. Then the bride's face turned into a glee-filled smile as she leaped forward to give him a long, loving hug.

Sometimes there are days with nothing to do but remember. To remember we made promises. To remember there are always some things we can do and there will always be things we can't quite do. When we got home after the wedding, we climbed into bed and I gave Pete a long, loving hug. That was my doing for the day.

Boys Meet Doctor

WE (PETE, I, AND BOTH OF OUR BOYS, DAN AND JOE) were on our way to see Pete's neurologist. If I remember correctly, we were bickering between the four of us on the merits of social media when I missed my turn. I rather loudly asked for everyone to stop talking so I could get us to the doctor's office. Silence fell over the car. Three more turns and then we were on our way down a familiar stretch of road when Pete broke the silence with his "dad voice." He said, "OK, here's what's gonna happen (pause for grander effect). Beth's going to pull up to the valet. One of you is going to get my rollator, the other is going to get the door." After a brief moment to process, the youngest says, "OK Dad, when it's time—just yell 'Go Team Red.' Still in his "dad voice," he said, "I will do no such thing." And yet just as I pulled up to the valet, Pete said "Go Team Red." Everyone jumped out, one with the door, the other with the Rollator, me handing over the keys, and in minutes we turned the corner to the neurology suite.

Until this point, I had resisted asking the boys to join us at doctor's appointments. They were not boys anymore, they were 34 and 29. They were independent young men. One with a family of his own and the other an able business manager. But I wanted them to be Pete's sons, not his caregivers. I wanted to shield them from some of the responsibility of caring for Pete's illness. That was my role.

I had not admitted to myself that perhaps I needed their care. It was possible that having them with me would alleviate some of my stress. I didn't want to admit that. I wanted to be able to do this on my own. I wanted to have all the resources on my own to take care of Pete. But they knew better. They knew I was running on empty. They knew I needed an extra pair of hands and an extra pair of ears. They had a lot to offer in terms of caring resources. Going to doctor's appointments were concrete help, too. Tangible help.

After one day of taking them to the doctor with me, I had learned my lesson. They were funny and clever and strong and smart. They were just what I needed. I didn't know how much I had been feeling alone in caring for Pete. It felt so good to have them with me. I spent years feeling weak when two of the strongest men I knew were a phone call away. I spent years trying to hold things together when together we were meant to hold one another.

BEING HUMAN

PETE DIDN'T LIKE TO THINK TOO FAR AHEAD. I, on the other hand, wanted to be prepared. When he was only sometimes using a walker, I wanted to take it with us—just in case. When we purchased the rollator (the walker that could transform into a transport wheelchair), he insisted on taking the walker, thinking he was strong enough that day. But then he would end up being too tired to manage with just the walker. I was constantly asking, "Don't you think we should...?"

Pete was and always had been a fairly stubborn man. I often would bring the extra device, ignoring Pete's answer. That often meant I packed double the assistive devices—just in case. As I packed the car, I took special care to slam every door along the way. All of this anger and irritation had to be about more than planning ahead or having to lug around extra devices. I was feeling ignored and underappreciated. I felt my opinion, my observations were not taken seriously, and my preparedness was taken for granted. I spent a lot of time caring for my partner. Our shared life had shifted in so many ways. I had different responsibilities now, more responsibilities. Pete required care now; there were things he could no longer do for himself. And although we tried to talk to one another, this was new territory for us. We weren't sure how to talk about what was happening to him, to me, to us.

I wanted so badly for Pete to acknowledge his limitations, but the truth was I was not acknowledging my own limitations. I was not taking care of myself. And I knew better. I knew that when I was rested and well fed, when I had exercised my body and employed some creativity, I had no problem managing our lives, including his illness, and even my career. But often I went without rest. I often went without protein. Many days I skipped the gym to watch the news. And then I would lose patience.

Grace would go out the window.

After such episodes of impatience and irritability, I would reboot with rest and protein but then a wave of shame would overtake me. I was ashamed that I had become a child who slams doors, ashamed that I had not taken care of myself while I asserted that I knew best how to take care of Pete, ashamed that I lacked patience and kindness. Pete's choice to take a certain device over another was his way of asserting his will, and a lot of the time he didn't get to assert his will. Our son Dan once said, "Whatever day I'm having, Dad's day is worse. We can get irritated with how he is responding to this disease, but we really can't imagine what it's like to live in his body." Dan was right. And Dan was also being patient and gracious.

Pete and I both hated the limitations of his body. He hated that the limitations of his body were causing changes to our lives. He felt to blame. He wished that he could just keep going even when his body had lost steam. I wished I could keep going even when my body had lost steam. We hated being limited by the human condition.

The human condition may have seemed limiting to us but the human condition is nothing short of astonishing. A colleague of mine gave a talk about our amazing human bodies. He asked, "Have you ever thought about how great our skin is? It's waterproof!" He's right. Our skin is also so very vulnerable. It bleeds when cut, burns in the sun and breaks out in hives when irritated. But its vulnerability is countered with its ability to heal itself. Systems in the body come to our assistance. We create scabs over cuts. Our body regulates its own temperature. We sneeze when faced with allergens. Being human is amazing and vulnerable and fascinatingly resilient.

The other thing about our skin is that it is our natural boundary. My skin contains me. Pete's skin contained him. When he asserted his will, when my patience wore thin, we were drawing boundaries between us. We had limits. We needed boundaries. Pete was allowed, entitled, welcomed to determine his own boundaries. When he pushed his limits, he was saying, "I'm am my own person." When Pete seemed to ignore his limitations, he was defining himself, essentially telling MS "you don't define me. You aren't me. You don't determine what or who I am" Being human was amazing and vulnerable and surprisingly resilient. And having limitations was something we were pushing against.

I Won the Lottery

NANCY'S HOUSE IS A NON-PROFIT OUTREACH that provides retreats and respite for caregivers. I almost couldn't believe it when I read the announcement that they were hosting a retreat for women who care for husbands who have MS. The majority of people who have MS are women, which means that the majority of spousal caregivers for those who have MS are men or husbands. Therefore, a retreat for women who cared for husbands with MS was like winning the lottery. I followed the link and emailed the MS Society, the organizing arm of the retreat. No response for a couple days. My friends encouraged me not to just wait for a response. Taking care of myself was important. So I felt like a stalker to both the MS representative and Elisa, the woman who runs Nancy's House. When I finally got the MS lady on the phone, she was so kind and happy that we had finally connected. She explained that there were only nine spots and that she had put my name on the list. I should receive a call from Nancy's House within the day.

An interesting thing almost happened before we hung up. I almost said "I appreciate you putting my name on the list but to be honest, my husband and I are doing very well, and he isn't that sick yet so if there is someone who needed this retreat more than me, please give it to her." After I hung up, I stopped to reflect why I would think such a thing! I guess I still wasn't completely convinced that I needed help. I hadn't resolved that I, the caregiver, needed care.

Then it happened. Elisa called and left a message. Her message said, "We hope that you will be able to join us at the caregiver retreat in a couple weeks from now. Please call to confirm." I felt like I had won the lottery. I called right back to confirm.

The conversation with Elissa included sentences like "I'm so glad you will be able to join us."

"Will you need help with home care for your spouse in order for you to join us?"

"Now remember this retreat is all about comfort—no dress up clothes, no high heels."

I was elated that I had won this lottery. I was also embarrassed to have been given a gift like this. I was anxious to meet others who had similar stories. I was so excited to be able to rest, to sleep without having to keep one ear open to listen for Pete in case he needed help.

I met eight wonderful women. Each was tired, just like me. Each was sad, just like me. Each was resilient, just like me.

After a glorious night of sleep, I woke early enough to take a leisurely walk with Elisa around the rolling green hills of the retreat center. Mid-morning the first day we learned breathing techniques to manage stress. In the afternoon I received a massage. Elisa had brought several books on caregiving, even a memoir or two written by caregivers for us to thumb through. The retreat was a wonderful mix of rest and resources.

Of course the best resource was conversation with one another. We listened to each other tell stories. Many of the stories for me offered a glimpse of what might be in my and Pete's future, both good and bad. Those stories reminded us of places we had been, good and bad. For example, I learned about a Hoyer lift, a mechanical swing that assists in transferring a person from one place to another. Most likely we would have one in our house at some point. I learned about a floor-to-ceiling grab bar that I purchased as soon as I got home. (Pete and the boys insisted on calling it a stripper pole. The pole was something sturdy for Pete to grab as he got in and out of the shower.)

The resources weren't limited to pragmatic ideas either. On the second morning, after meditation, we were lingering, and one woman shared an intimate story with us. She and her husband had recently purchased an accessible bathtub big enough for both of them. She told us a story of how they had recently bathed one another. Not only was it intimate but the intimacy was reciprocal. Our eyes were fixed on her, joyful for what she and her husband had found. When she was finished, others shared about the difficulties of intimacy, the awkwardness, the frustration, the pain, the felt rejection, the shame. This community, this sacred circle had created sanctuary for one another. We stood, sat, knelt, shared, cried, listened on holy ground.

There were others just like me, whose lives had been invaded by the outsider: MS. There were others who had experienced trauma. There were others whose lives were filled with the chaos of chronic illness. There were others who grieved every day little losses and big dreams. I was not alone.

REALLY VERY SMALL

A FEW MONTHS AFTER THE CAREGIVERS' RETREAT, the high of the retreat was gone, and I was back to having a hard time sleeping. I felt alone again. One night I went to bed early and as I laid there considering prayer. I say "considering" because I wasn't sure how to start the prayer. I sort of hoped God would start the conversation; after all prayer is as much listening as it is talking to God, whatever and whomever God is. For me, prayer was not meditation in the strict sense. We usually associate prayer with words and meditation with silence, although prayer can be silent and meditation can use mantras which are words. I wanted a conversation with God but I didn't know how to start it.

So often I prayed for healing, understanding, comfort, release from guilt, shame, or worry. Sometimes I received the things for which I asked. Sometimes I did not. I had prayed for Pete's healing. Others had prayed for Pete's healing. Yet Pete still had MS. I had prayed to be a more compassionate person. And truly, from my standpoint, I had the same amount of compassion I always had. I really struggled with compassion...and patience and kindness and self-control. The whole ordeal of his illness was shining light on so many areas of my life that could grow. So what was there different to pray? What was prayer supposed to be or do? What was God supposed to be or do?

A friend and colleague of mine, Michael, had recently said that he was "holding out for a postmodern definition of God." He, like so many of my colleagues and friends, had struggled with the traditional definition of God. I certainly had, too. What would a postmodern definition of God be? We know what it wouldn't be. It wouldn't be the "man upstairs." It would most certainly not be the bearded, half-naked dude on the ceiling of the Sistine Chapel, the one who reaches toward us with strangely muscular arms for an old man. It wouldn't be a cosmic police officer either, ready to pull us over when we've broken the law, give us a summons, or declare us guilty and demand payment in the form of confession, good works, and change of behavior. It also wouldn't be the beloved uncle figure (or aunt if you like me are beginning to be irritated by the male images) who always listens, always cares, and provides a different support than that of your parents or friends. The man upstairs, the police officer, the beloved aunt—they all were falling short of a postmodern definition of "God."

So as I laid there considering prayer, my struggle was less about finding the words and more about wondering who I was talking to. I've always quoted Mark Twain as saying "God made man in his own image and man, being fair minded, returned the favor." It turns out Mark Twain didn't say that. Blaise Pascal did. Blaise Pascal was the mathematician/physicist turned theologian/writer. After he invented the calculator, he wrote a defense for God in a series of letters that were burned by the Catholic church in the mid-1600's. I believe the first thing I was taught about Pascal though was his "wager." Pascal's wager goes something like this: Some people may not be willing to sincerely believe in God even after acknowledging that there is an enormous benefit of betting in favor of God's existence. If that is the case, then Pascal advises to live as though one has faith, which may overcome passions and lead to genuine belief.

My quick interpretation of Pascal's wager: Fake it 'til you make it. But as I laid there in bed, I was not satisfied with Pascal's encouragement to fake it until I made it. So there I was still lying in bed considering prayer when Pete showed up and said, "You okay?"

I said, "Yeah, I'm just considering prayer."

"Considering it, huh? What is there to consider?"

I told him I was a bit melancholy. Then I asked him what he thought happens when we pray. And his answer would have made Pascal proud. He said, "I don't know, but I still do it." I told him that the act of prayer wasn't the problem, I had no problem "talking" but who was I talking to? What was I talking to? I wasn't really sure what or who God was anymore. If prayer was a conversation tool, then who or what was on the other end? And the more I thought of God as the creative force of the universe, the first mover, the energy that connects us all, the less the term "God" seemed appropriate because I was no longer talking about the same thing other people were talking about when they talked about "God."

Being a pastor and being his caregiver had added so many new experiences to my life. My definition, my picture of God had been challenged. There were so many problems, so many hurts in the world. At best, I was looking through "soft eyes" hoping for some peripheral vision or clarity. But my sight wasn't clear. The world had become fuzzy. As if my understanding of God was changing. The definition itself was in flux, in motion; it had not settled yet. Wouldn't it make sense that as my understanding of God changed, so must my way of relating to God? And since I wasn't quite sure who or what I was talking to, I laid there in the dark, considering prayer.

Pete listened to me faithfully and lovingly. He asked if I had these questions before becoming a pastor. He told me that I knew the job would be hard on my spiritual life. He reminded me that I had seen and experienced difficult situations. I would continue to see and experience difficult situations. So, "really," he asked, "what's this about?"

After a pause, I said, "I got small."

We saw Esperanza Spalding in concert earlier that year. Before she sang her song "Really, Very Small," she scatted out a poem, a monologue that went something like this,

> There once was a little girl
> Who was told she was a really big deal
> And she started to believe it...
> But after a while,
> that little girl realized we are really very small.

That's what was happening to me—I had been told for a very long time that I was sort of a big deal. I had wonderful gifts. I was a gifted singer, speaker, writer. I was a great friend. But the world—the world has turned out to be enormous. The stars we see twinkling in the sky were relatives of our sun. The oak tree outside my house has withstood rain, sleet, snow, hurricanes. It has dropped thousands of tiny acorns each year and has grown yet another ring with seeming ease. Thousands of people each day live through abuse, turmoil. Girls have been sold into slavery. Every day people lose hope in love—for family, for spouse, or for brother or sister. Parents have lost a child, by nature or by accident, and have never fully recovered from that trauma.

We fight the bad of life with poison, in the case of cancer or interferon in the case of MS. We fight but our ammunition is inferior to the forces that assault us. If we can't fight the bad, we fill our lives with more and more, pushing the bad into corners in hopes we can't see it or feel it anymore. But the bad is happy to live in the corners of our lives. The bad, the sick, the sad, will happily take up permanent residency in as much space as it can get.

I wanted to consider giving in. What if I stopped fighting? What if we would lay down our ammunition and accept human frailty as a permanent condition? I was vulnerable, weak, hurting. I was not so big after all. I was really, very small.

I learned a pose in yoga, a yoga mudra. The position calls us to sit cross-legged, arms behind the back, one hand wrapped around the other wrist. Then fold the torso over the legs and let the mind go deep inside. Each time I have done this pose I have always been struck by how very small I could make myself. And my mind was able to focus on an even smaller part of me. The me inside me. It was the me inside me that was lying in bed that night considering prayer.

MY PRAYER I A SIGH

I was finding great solace in the Psalms. They are so very human and honest, vulnerable and rich. Since I didn't know how to pray at the time, these ancient writers shared their prayers with me—prayers of praise, of lament, of thanks, of worry. But sometimes their words didn't work either.

Sigh.

And then I found this psalm, "*All our days pass away under your wrath; our years come to an end like a sigh.*" (Psalm 90.9) The wrath of God? My days pass under the wrath of God? that seemed pretty harsh. Although my life seemed fairly wrath-filled at times. Perhaps wrath was accurate. But I was not willing to define God as wrathful.

It was possible I didn't understand wrath. Perhaps wrath was more about boundaries between the infinite and the finite world. After all, we clock our days with calendars whereas God lives outside of time. We use our five senses to understand the world whereas God isn't limited by any of those senses. What if the wrath of God was simply the felt disconnect between the infinite world and the finite world? What if the "wrath of God" was another way of saying "I've come up against a hard limit?" We don't really like hard limits. We don't like imposed boundaries.

My life had a lot of imposed boundaries it seemed. Physical boundaries like how many hours were in the day. Boundaries of illness like how Pete was able to move on any particular day. My life was filled with imposed boundaries, boundaries that I had not erected. I was in control of so little it seemed. The world did not work the way I wanted or hoped, even if I did all the right things all the time. My life was finite, limited in its breadth and understanding. I had an end. Pete had an end.

Sigh.

The psalmist seemed to be having one of those days when

life on earth had run into a boundary.

Sigh.

The psalmist was in that thin space where he or she must face the reality that God is really not us, and that we are really not God.

Sigh.

I was sighing. Sometimes in relief. Sometimes in exhaustion. Sometimes in disgust. Sometimes in defeat.

My sigh was a prayer. The psalmist was onto something.

BLUE MOON

IT WAS NEW YEAR'S EVE, and there was going to be a blue moon. Apparently there was an extra moon cycle in 2009, and that extra moon was called a "blue moon" and it happens...once in a blue moon. The last time it shined on New Year's Eve was in 1990, and the next time would be in 2028.

The term "once in a blue moon" obviously meant "something unlikely to happen." A blue moon had nothing to do with the color of the moon, except that "once in a blue moon" the moon also appeared to be blue. And I had gotten fixated on the upcoming blue moon.

I was fixated on the unlikeliness of it. I was living with so many things that would never happen. Pete would never be able to hold a cup steady. Pete would never be able to dance with me. Pete would never be able to drive me around. Never. I was facing a lot of never. Yet there were things in the world that were rare like the blue moon. Things we thought were unlikely to never happen sometimes happened.

If the rare blue moon appears, then can I, a person who believes in the creator of the blue moon, open myself to other rarities? If the blue moon is actually something that does from time to time happen, albeit few and far between, then maybe there was hope for the other rarities for which I wished and prayed. Maybe Pete could one day hold a cup steady. Maybe one day we could dance again. Maybe he could get better.

There were people in our lives who prayed for Pete's healing every day. I no longer prayed for healing in that way. I had decided instead to pray for peace as I managed his care. I prayed that Pete and I would be kind to one another. I prayed for sleep for me and for Pete. I prayed for Pete not to fall. I prayed for wisdom in our choices and courage in our living. All of these prayers were somehow within the realm of human control or self-control. They were not far-fetched or unlikely. I had stopped believing in the unlikely. I had stopped believing in things like a blue moon. And yet the blue moon was about to happen.

DARKNESS

IN SO MANY WAYS, AS I WALKED THROUGH THIS JOURNEY with Pete's MS diagnosis, I referred back to the experience I had with Jean who died from ALS. It had been one of the primary learning stories as a pastor so far. Jean was on my search committee, the group of people who interview potential pastors for their church. Jean was the first to call me at my home. We quickly found many things to talk about. She had been a classics major in undergrad so she was very interested in my studies in seminary. She went on to teach middle school students so she wanted to talk about my sermons. She was retired at this point; she enjoyed reading and gardening. She had two large, gray poodles who I would later find out were trained as therapy dogs. The older was a bit better at visiting people in the hospital; she was more docile in nature. But the younger, rambunctious one brought the liveliness that many in the nursing home enjoyed. Jean was a breast cancer survivor who found many ways to give back. The decision to train her dogs as therapy dogs was one way that she could serve people who were experiencing a darker time in their lives. She was not afraid of darkness; after all, she had walked through darkness herself.

She mentored other women going through cancer treatment, and she spoke at cancer support groups. The first thing I noticed about Jean was her speech pattern. She spoke intentionally with a little rasp in her voice. She spoke slowly—very slowly as if she had a hard time getting the words out. Listening in general takes patience but for Jean, listening took a tad bit more patience.

Jean was a church person. Her parents raised her in the Baptist tradition and she knew her way around the Bible really well. But with her knowledge of the classics, she also knew her way around mythology and world religions. She was the leader of one of the small groups at our church. They had read Marcus

Borg, an American New Testament scholar who was a prominent influential voice in progressive Christianity. They read Alane Pagel, a religious historian who wrote the most prominent, accessible book on the Gnostic gospels, a collection of early Christian texts discovered in Upper Egypt in 1945. They read Jim Wallis, a Christian writer, political activist and founder of the widely popular social justice magazine *Sojourners*. This small group at our church was definitely an interesting mix of people who learned with one another and from one another. Jean and I spoke often about our theological journeys. After all, I, too, had traveled from the Baptist world to the Presbyterian world.

On Sunday mornings Jean and her husband Charlie sat to my right about seven pews back on the side aisle. Always ready to worship, always quick to encourage, and always ready to help out. She had served as an elder for years. She had served a variety of committees. But before her diagnosis with ALS, she had found that her experience with cancer was drawing her into conversations with people around her who were experiencing their own journey with darkness. Jean had accepted a nomination to be ordained as a Deacon right around the time that I became her pastor.

I had hopes for the Deacon Board. I wanted them to begin providing more intentional pastoral care with me. Jean was fantastic help in organizing the Deacons in this direction. She was a strong leader, some might say strong-headed. And yet to look at her, she was a tiny woman, almost feeble...until, of course, she opened her mouth to share her opinion. She had short, salt and pepper hair that was always styled. She enjoyed make-up and jewelry, and so a pair of faded jeans was paired with a yellow and blue long-sleeved cotton top that was matched with a chunky silver necklace and matching earrings. She wore glasses and had caring, serious, blue eyes decorated with a tasteful amount of mascara and eye liner.

She set about in her own style to rework the Board of Deacons, organizing the "families" in the church so as to provide optimal care. She balanced the more difficult situations, meaning those who were facing particular darkness, among the Deacons so that members were receiving optimal care. Each Deacon connected with about 15 people in the congregation, and between two to five of the people on their list might be experiencing some situation that required more care from the Deacon. For example, one woman's elderly father had recently died, and she was grieving. Another family had their only child head off to school and they, too, were grieving. One member had cancer, another had chronic depression, yet another, fibromayalgia. And then of course there was one woman who happened to be the pastor, had a husband with MS. Yep, I was on the list. The Deacons were caring for me, too. Jean's organizational skills were unmatched, and she ran the Deacon Board like a Swiss watch—until she was diagnosed with ALS.

From the ALS Association's website:[2]

Amyotrophic lateral sclerosis (ALS), often referred to as "Lou Gehrig's Disease," is a progressive neurodegenerative disease that affects nerve cells in the brain and the spinal cord. Motor neurons reach from the brain to the spinal cord and from the spinal cord to the muscles throughout the body. The progressive degeneration of the motor neurons in ALS eventually leads to their death. When the motor neurons die, the ability of the brain to initiate and control muscle movement is lost. With voluntary muscle action progressively affected, patients in the later stages of the disease may become totally paralyzed. A-myo-trophic comes from the Greek language. "A" means no or negative. "Myo" refers to muscle, and "Trophic" means nourishment, "No muscle nourishment."

She was devastated; we were devastated. What was she about to go through? What care did she need from me? What did she need from her community of faith? None of those questions could be answered by the internet. All of those questions needed to be opened, and answered, in conversation.

[2] http://www.alsa.org/about-als/what-is-als.html

I visited her at her home. She lived on a dead-end street in Hillsborough, just across the canal from church. She asked if I had come over on the one-lane bridge. She loved to tell people how angry she was that they tore down that one-lane bridge and then replaced it with another one-lane bridge. She escorted me to their glass-enclosed patio—clearly her favorite room in the house. She sat on the couch, and I sat in the flowered chair opposite her. We were surrounded by 30 plants that she had tended with her own hands, her own feeble, shaky hands that now produced horrible penmanship. When I sat down, I noticed she had a list beside her chair that read:

tomatoes

garlic

book group

Beth—why me

pills

"Jean, how are you?" I asked.

She began to cry and that was the end of any talking that day. I moved to sit beside her on the couch; I held her hand while she cried. Occasionally, she looked out the window, attempted to fight back tears and find words. But the tears won. Instead of words, she reached for another tissue and I squeezed her hand or rubbed her back.

She had fed her body with the best organic produce. She had exercised religiously. She had prayed vigorously. She had read voraciously. And now her body was no longer nourishing her muscles. I was holding one of her hands and I could feel the lack of form between her thumb and forefinger. There was darkness in her hand. There was darkness in her life. I began to cry too. Sometimes when I spend time with people who are suffering, I never want to leave people in the dark alone. She gave me a cue when she said, still with tears in her eyes, "I'm gonna get started on dinner." I kissed her lightly on her forehead and said I'd see her on Sunday.

"I love you, Jean."

"I love you, too," she said.

Mauve Carpet

Our master bedroom had a 1985 mauve carpet. In fact the majority of the house was that color for the first five years we lived there. I had a love/hate relationship with the color. My teenage bedroom had that same color carpet. Of course, it was actually 1985 back then. It was no longer 1985. In fact, it was more than two decades later, but the decorative sensibilities of our home were primarily driven by the color mauve.

I tried to cover up the mauve with as much navy as I could. A navy quilt commissioned by my bridesmaids (more than 10 years earlier) covered our bed. The quilt was splashed with various prints of pink flowers with white and green accents. Our headboard was a textured, faux suede with the same rich blue.

To the right of our bed was a large space that I used as a dressing area, essentially. My closet, complete with mirrored doors, was where I had my almost daily fashion crisis. I am one of those people who rarely settles on the first outfit I put on. Sometimes after I brush my teeth and do my hair, the outfit I had chosen simply doesn't seem "right" for the day. So I find another.

On this spot of mauve carpet, in front of the mirrors, was where I found my bearings each day. This spot of carpet was about four feet by eight feet, and it was well-worn. In fact, I often sat down on that piece of carpet, to think, to pray, to cry. Although that 32-foot square piece of ground wasn't enclosed, it was my "closet." Jesus talks about going into our "inner room" to pray. "Shut the door behind you" when you pray. There was no door to this "closet" space but it was my piece of hallowed ground where I enjoyed a few moments alone every single day. This was where I took my emotional and spiritual temperature. It was this small piece of ground where I gathered my thoughts. On this mauve-colored carpet, I pulled myself together each day. I considered what was before me, what was to be done, what would most likely be left undone. It was here where I collected myself.

One morning I came home from the gym to an empty house. Pete had gone to work and in the quiet, I found sacred space to think about what was happening to us, well—to him. No, to us. At that time he had just shifted from a walking stick to a walker. The walker was a navy color with a black seat that folded down when he needed to rest. He needed to rest a lot lately. Fatigue was the most common symptom of his multiple sclerosis. He was tired all the time. Pete wasn't cranky like I certainly would have been. He was rarely impatient. He was however forgetful. He was starting to have difficulty remembering what needed to be done or where we needed to be at what time. He seemed to be avoiding some of this reality by spending a lot of time on his laptop. In fact, his avoidance sometimes seemed as if he left me and went to another place, just for him. I was missing him.

When I realized I was missing him, I was sitting cross-legged on my mauve carpet in my sacred space. I was thinking about how multiple sclerosis had moved into our house and was taking up so much space. But MS hadn't taken over this hallowed ground. And there on the mauve carpet, I began to cry. My crying became sobbing—the snotty kind of sobbing. I laid down in my "closet" and was running my hands over the mauve carpet, picking at it. And then my hand pulled up a four-inch square piece of the carpet. I sat up, sniffled and stared at the chunk of mauve carpet.

I had cried a hole in my carpet.

How long had I cried in this holy space? How long had my tears dripped on this piece of carpet? How many days had I been on my knees hoping that my tears would render a prayer, a prayer that would change my circumstances, our circumstances? For the love of God, now there was a hole in the carpet.

I laid down again, down, facing the mirrors. My puffy, pink face looked back at me. I will never forget the feel of that soft, albeit a little itchy mauve carpet. That carpet held me when I was alone. That carpet supported me when I collected myself, fashion crisis after fashion crisis. That carpet was my witness and it now it had a hole in it.

WHISTLING IN THE DARK

I was starting to dwell on the "can'ts" of my life. Or, more correctly, the "can'ts" of Pete's life. Pete can't drive. Pete can't carry things across the room, like a cup of coffee or our granddaughter, Julia. Pete can't take pictures because his hands are too shaky. Pete can walk but not too far; Pete can't walk to the restroom at the movie theater. Pete can't walk on the beach.

These little losses were creating a growing darkness in our lives. The losses weren't just to his body, but to how we related to one another. At the end of almost every workday, Pete used to come up behind me in the kitchen, turn me around and we would dance together in silence. We couldn't do that anymore. The light that once was created by that moment had been snuffed out. Pete couldn't open the door for me anymore; a small loss that took a little bit more light from our lives. Pete couldn't help carry the groceries inside from the car. Less light. Pete couldn't run errands. Less light. Pete couldn't hug me while standing up. The darkness was getting so hard to navigate.

I believed a portion of the darkness was also created by our lack of ability to talk about what was happening. I didn't want to hurt him by talking about all the things he could no longer do. I wished he would give some direction about how we should proceed. I wanted to follow his lead as he learned how to navigate the darkness of his body. I didn't want to be in charge of getting through the darkness of our new normal. And while I didn't want to hurt his feelings, not talking to him about things left me feeling isolated. By withholding my feelings, I was adding to the darkness between us.

The darker our lives got, the harder I found his illness and our relationship to navigate. It was at this point that I stumbled upon a book by Matthew Sanford called *Waking*. When Matthew Sanford was 13 years old, he was in a devastating car accident that killed his father and sister and left him paralyzed from the neck down. After he regained consciousness, his surviving mother and brother explained what had happened. Here is how he describes his mind responding to the news of the trauma:

> *I could not control what was going to happen, but I could control how I perceived my situation. I needed to find a path, a way to keep going forward. So, I told myself a story, a healing story—my mother and brother needed me to live. [My healing story] was like whistling in the dark, a way to feel rhythm despite being engulfed in the unknown.[3]*

I wanted to tell myself a healing story. I wanted to reframe my life, reframe the changes happening to Pete's body and to our marriage. But the world felt so dark; I couldn't see well enough to reframe anything. Matthew Sanford was paralyzed from the chest down. He began creating his healing story by listening to his body. But his body was silent. He said listening to his body was like walking through a dark room. When we first enter a dark room, we have to allow our eyes to adjust. And they do; our eyes adjust. We adjust. And then when we can see just enough to cross the room, we take a step.

I heard Sanford encouraging me to listen to the darkness in our lives. Listen to the silence that is found in the darkness. Sit with the silence long enough for my eyes, my physical sight as well as my emotional understanding, to adjust to the darkness. There was light, he said, even in darkness. Give it time. Be patient with the darkness. We would be able to cross through this dark place.

I knew I definitely couldn't walk through the darkness alone. Pete and I needed to do this together. We needed to face the realities around us. We needed to talk about the darkness, which was uncomfortable and difficult. He needed to name his obstacles. I need to own up to my frustration and impatience. We needed to describe the darkness to one another. And when we

---

[3] Sanford, Matthew, *Waking: A Memoir of Trauma and Transcendence.* Rodale Books 2004, page 232.

described the darkness, Sanfords said our eyes would adjust. Our eyes would begin to see the light that we thought had been snuffed out by the darkness of disease and change. I believed this. I believed that we might just be able to see our way across or through the darkness that MS had created. I believed my eyes, my life, my heart would adjust and perhaps even find acceptance.

Acceptance wasn't going to happen all at once with a progressive disease. Acceptance was going to be the result of daily discipline. After all, every day presented its own challenges, with or without multiple sclerosis. Each new challenge required a new adjustment. We were not going to accept our new normal "once and for all." We were going to accept one thing at a time; we were going to have to walk through the dark one step at a time. And we were walking together; this could not be my own singular journey. We needed courage to face the darkness and faith to believe there would be enough light to help us cross through the it.

One August, while vacationing with my dad and stepmother, we attended the Keystone Blues and Arts Festival. We sat surrounded by the Rocky Mountains; us in lawn chairs and Pete in his rollator. A rollator is a walker that when turned around becomes a transport wheelchair. At this stage of Pete's illness, a rollator was the perfect device. He could walk when he was able but when he ran out of steam, someone could push him. We bought some wine and chocolate and settled into the haunting, longing sounds of the blues. About halfway through the afternoon, we saw a woman slowly moving through the crowd toward us. Her left foot was in a cast and she was using a basic walker, two small front wheels with back sliders. When she arrived closer to us, she stopped to catch her breath. Pete caught a glimpse of her and motioned to me. He pointed to his chair and then to the woman and then to me. He stopped her and offered her the use of his rollator. She paused, but then smiled and said confidently, "Yes."

People with disabilities often go unseen. We can make some philosophical conclusion, like humans don't want to face life's brokenness, but it might be more pragmatic than that. We may overlook folks because we are walking faster or we're not at the same eye level. It may be more like what Sanford was talking about when he said our eyes adjust when we cross the darkness. Pete and I had spent a lot of time crossing the darkness. Our eyes had begun to adjust, and we saw others who were in the darkness with us. Others we may not have seen save illness.

Pete transferred to my lawn chair and our new friend Sandra, sat down in Pete's rollator. Once Sandra was settled, she looked at me and said, "How do I make it go?" I said, "I push you." She said, "You come with it too?!" And we were off on our journey to the restrooms. There were 150 feet more to go in this world of darkness, of multiple sclerosis and rollators, of casts and walkers. But we were seeing through it just fine.

ANGER

MY FAMILY DOES ANGER PRETTY WELL. Pete's family does not. Pete swore that his parents never fought in front of him. I remembered enough family fights to channel a variety of people when I fought. In the movie *Jerry Maguire,* Jerry and Rod Tidwell are talking loudly. Jerry starts to walk away and Rod says, "See Jerry, you think we're fighting and I think we're finally talking." That sums up my belief on loud conversation.

It wasn't not just about being loud or being angry. I had always tended to run a little hot. Whenever I walk into a room, I have a story to tell. I get excited. I use the word "fabulous" a lot. I have a large personality. When Pete and I were dating, my mother was describing Pete to my grandmother, her mother. She said, "Pete is so wonderfully peaceful. He's really a calming presence for Beth." My grandmother responded, "Well that's a good thing because sometimes you gotta scrape Beth off the walls."

That's what I mean when I say that I tended to "run hot." Pete—he did not.

There were many days when the darkness we were navigating was too much to add to the other stresses of life. For example, I remember prepping for a funeral. I was sad for the family who was experiencing loss. I was praying for some difficult dynamics in the family. I wanted my homily to provide helpful pastoral care. On top of the funeral, there were a few people at church who needed my emotional attention. And my emotional well was running dry.

Of course, on the back burners, the stresses related to Pete's illness were always on a soft boil. That week in particular we were considering a new drug on the market that might have helped Pete. Add to that, we had offered to babysit our grandchild, a complete joy, but another thing for which to carve out time and energy. I had reached a limit to how much grocery shopping, cooking, cleaning I could do. And the laundry—my God—it never stopped. I had bought a new kind of coffee and it was just awful. And good Lord, I needed a haircut.

I looked in the mirror and said, "You look like someone who doesn't care about herself." It wasn't just my physical appearance; my emotional needs had been put to the side after we had tried to pull together a family dinner but couldn't settle on a night. I was so emotionally drained that all of this sent me into a mini-pity party. I mean, "If I didn't care about myself, why should anyone else?"

Stress was building up inside of me. A walk outside would've helped, but it was so hot outside. In fact, it had been hot for three weeks. You know the public service announcement "elderly and people with chronic illnesses should stay out of the heat?" Well, Pete qualified now. They were talking about him. He shouldn't go out in the heat. And so he hadn't. I had ordered a few new books that were sitting on the table as a reminder that while I used to be an avid reader, my attention span had dwindled, making the last book I read in its entirety, *Goodnight Moon.*

As the stress was building, the irritation was…well… irritating me, I tried not to sweat the small stuff but wasn't life just a lot of small stuff that when put together makes up one big thing we like to call "life?"

As I was holding in my frustration, my pity party, I was playing one morning with our granddaughter, Julia. She was fussy, and our family started talking about "fussiness." Dan, her dad, said, "If you think about it, how many times a day do you complain or moan about small stuff? She doesn't have words yet so her fussiness is probably her just saying 'it's hot,' or 'I don't want to do that anymore,' or 'where's my book,' or 'how come I can't find the pink ball?'"

Yes! Yes! Julia was sweating the small stuff by being fussy. But fussiness was unacceptable as an adult. So what was I doing instead of being fussy? I was sweating the small stuff. We all sweat the small stuff. Sweating the small stuff was natural; it was a natural human response. There was nothing wrong with me. I wasn't failing at carrying the stresses of my life. I was normal.

Fussiness was, and is, a natural human response.

Now of course, grownups don't moan or grunt. We have been taught to use our words and to do so with indoor voices. But seriously, indoor voices sometimes just didn't do my emotions justice. And besides, what's so wrong with outside voices?

Well, being someone who liked her outdoor voice and someone who had used it a lot—particularly with her husband who had a chronic illness—the problem with outdoor voices was that we had to live with ourselves after using them. We can only afford to yell at those who love us the most because we trust they will love us still. And even though I knew Pete continued to love me, I still felt a horrible sense of shame after I had used my outside voice in conversation with him. A little voice inside me would ask me, "Who yells at a sick person?"

You know who? A lot of people. Humans yell. Humans get fussy. Humans stress out.

Yes. Yes. But why? Why was I yelling? If it was fussiness, if I was indeed sweating the small stuff, certainly some of the small stuff could be dealt with.

I felt like a spider who had created a web with every small stress, every small irritation. I was tired. I was hungry. I wanted someone else to make dinner. I wanted a night off. I wanted to do nothing but watch mindless television. Or maybe I wanted to go on a date—a real date where we stayed out later and danced and laughed. But I was too tired for any of that. And so I wove my web and I crawled up into the corner of it until I sat high above the rest of my life.

I could see it all: my whole pitiful life. I had clarity; and by clarity I mean the kind of clarity a person has when they have gone crazy with anger. My mind was spinning with anger and I knew I would not be able to get myself down from this perch. So I called a friend from my acidic perch, and I asked her in a crazed voice, "Please help me down from here." She asked me, "How did you get up there?" I told her. Then she asked, "What do you see?" And I told her. She listened to every grievance, every stress, every irritant, every disappointment. She listened until she could see the web as clearly as me. Once I knew I had been heard, I started to descend. But then I remembered everything that was "down there." If I descended, I had to face it all again. Whereas "up here," protected by my anger, I was free. I was separate. I was alone. And so, I stopped and asked her, "Rather than me come down, would you like to come up?" And when she paused, most certainly determining what she wanted to say, I added, "They're serving Mai Tais up here."

She tried a new question, "What one or two things could we do to alleviate the stress, wipe away the irritants or fix the disappointments?" Together we came up with four things:

I would schedule a haircut.

I would begin reading one of the books even if it didn't keep my attention.

I would ask Pete to do the laundry.

I would ask Pete to schedule a date—a real date, out of the house, one that included a fancy meal.

Anger is not something to avoid or ignore. Anger collects data. When I stopped long enough to listen to my anger, I learned what I needed. And for me, anger often hosted other emotions. Behind my anger was vulnerability, sadness and fear.

Anger was guiding me. When I listened to my anger, it showed me the way forward. Anger was what guided me to solutions.

Things to Do in Water

I SWAM COMPETITIVELY IN HIGH SCHOOL. My favorite event was the 200-meter freestyle, not a sprint but not really a distance race either. In this event the goal was always to find a steady, fast-paced stride. In so many ways that event describes the life I wished I had. I wished my life could maintain a steady fast-paced stride. I tried to keep my life steady and fast-paced by planning ahead, keeping a calendar active. An active calendar is neither filled with spurts of too much energy nor does it have periods of inactivity.

I was a list keeper. I kept lots of lists. I had your basic shopping list, a to-do list, a list of ideas for writing, a list with ideas for up upcoming sermons, a list of Pete's medical needs and/or medications, a list of random stuff I need to keep track of. Between the calendar and my lists, I had kept my life moving in a steady, fast-paced stride. I was succeeding in living my life like a 200-meter freestyle race.

But MS stopped all of that. People who live with chronic illness move neither steady nor fast-paced.

But it wasn't only chronic illness that had interrupted my stride—being the pastor of a church was also making it hard to keep a steady, fast-paced stride. I had chosen to walk with other people and when we choose to walk together, our strides get wonky. Sometimes we ran into each other. Sometimes we trip on each other. And sure, sometimes our strides began to match. But the only way that happened was when those with faster paces slowed down and/or those with slower paces sped up. If I insisted on keeping my stride, my steady, fast-paced stride, I was going to end up walking alone.

I married with the intent of having a partner. I needed to adjust my stride so that I was walking alongside him. If I truly wanted to share my life with someone, if I wanted others to share their lives with me, if I wanted to play together and think together, love together, and learn together, then my stride needed to adjust. And even with adjustments, I needed to accept interruptions, bumps, trips were going to happen.

I didn't like this at all, but this was the price to pay in order to be in relationship with others. I could have chosen not to pay the price. I could have given in to my selfishness and then my selfishness would have been what kept me from living in relationships. I could have insisted on my way, in my time. And I could have blamed the whole thing on others who couldn't keep up. I could have blamed multiple sclerosis. I could have blamed marriage for that matter. Pete and I were most certainly not the same person, nor did we even enjoy walking through life at the same pace. We didn't have the same stride, nor did we have the same hope for how much ground we would cover over the course of our marriage. I think I was learning simply to let my expectations go.

I chose to adjust my stride to match others around me. And one day when I was on vacation in Colorado, I dropped the stride altogether and I floated. I was in an outdoor, heated pool, surrounded by mountains and Aspen trees. I stopped trying and I floated.

I had forgotten how fun it was to float. Floating was just a matter of air. When I filled my body with air, I rose to the surface of the water. As I exhaled, my body sank just below the surface of the water. When I inhaled, floating was easier. On the exhale I had to adjust my core muscles to keep afloat. In and out, rise and fall. In and out, rise and fall. I was floating. It was so quiet. My ears were under water and I heard myself breathing. The voices of others around the pool were muffled. I was in my own space, the mountains, the aspens, an occasional bird who incidentally was also floating on air of course, rather than water.

Just before vacation, one of my colleagues had shared with me about her search for another job. She had been working primarily as an interim pastor, meaning she guided churches while they were transitioning from one pastor to another. She typically stayed at a church for three years. She had been here before—in between jobs. But each time was still an exercise in trusting God. She was always a little scared, but she had learned to "float," she said.

All too often I chose to tread water rather than float. I chose to move my arms back and forth, bicycle my legs round and round. In high school when we were in between swimming seasons, we played water polo for fun. I hated it. The ball only moved through three or four hands before someone tried to score. Most of the game was spent treading water. It was exhausting and I found it boring.

Then why when life was interrupted, was I choosing the same kind of exhausting, boring activity? My "treading water" took the form of adding other activities or finding other things to do that filled up my schedule. Or I looked ahead and tried to plan as best as I could trying to avoid having to stop. I tried to do anything to keep from stopping, anything to stay moving, anything—except floating.

Swimming through life at a steady, fast-paced stride was not going to happen. I could spend my energy treading water when life's stride tripped or when life stuttered to a halt. Or I could stop with it. I could take a deep breath in and watch myself float. I loved to swim. I hated to tread water. I was learning to float.

INTERCONNECTED LIVES

A MAN IN MY CONGREGATION DIED. He had been caring for his wife who had Alzheimer's. Along the way he had modeled for me and my congregation an admirable kind of love. When his wife first became ill, he cared for her as long as he could in their home. They lived in a retirement community that had step-down units, if and when needed. He dealt with so many little losses along the way. A loss of communication, a loss of mobility, a loss of activity, a loss of time, a loss of conversation, a loss of shared life. When her disease progressed he realized she would be safer sleeping in the nursing unit. He also realized he would get a better night's sleep. But each morning he would go to the nursing facility, pick her up, take her to exercise, then to lunch and then back to the apartment for the afternoon. In the evening, he brought her back to the nursing facility and the next day started all over again.

One day he approached one of our Deacons to ask her opinion about taking a day off from caring for his wife. He was so ashamed at even the thought of it. He felt like a failure. How could he not have had enough energy to take care of his best friend and life partner? I bet he remembered the lunches that she packed for him when he commuted to the city or how she worked full time and raised their children. I wondered if he cataloged the special dinners she prepared or the way she made their earlier life so beautiful.

We encouraged him to take time off. We encouraged him to be human. We told him that his wife would want that for him. She would want for him to take care of himself. Eventually, he adjusted his expectations of himself. He took one day off. And then he started to take one day each week, sometimes even two. He hurt his back lifting her and two days became three. And then one day he caught a cold. And then he died. We didn't see it coming.

His children had made the difficult decision to hold a memorial service for their father but chose to have their mother not attend. She had recently taken a fall and was in pain herself. None of us were certain whether or not she understood that her husband had died. We all wondered how she was going to respond to so many family and friends visiting her. The whole situation was sad and complicated.

Her husband had set the bar so high for me as a caregiver. His faithfulness inspired me. His need for a break instructed me. And although his story was not my story, nor was mine his, my life was so much richer for knowing him. My struggle as a pastor has always been to differentiate myself from those under my care. While I was struggling as a caregiver, I often left a pastoral care visit, sat in my car, keys in hand but not quite ready to turn the ignition. I needed to distinguish their suffering from mine. Our struggles were not the same, but they uniquely connected us in beautiful, life-giving ways.

Suffering in life so often acts like connective tissue tethering us to one another so that we do not feel as though we are alone. Sometimes the tethers seemed too real, too burdensome, too messy. Sometimes the tethers were lifelines. This man's example of love proved a lifeline for me—a connection to someone else who knew loss, someone who adjusted expectations but only let go in death.

THINGS THAT GROW

WHEN I WAS MEETING WITH HIS FAMILY to plan the funeral service, they asked if I wanted to take any of his plants home. Of course I did! I chose a succulent with thick green leaves. At the time it had five vertical stalks with many little baby stalks waiting underneath for room to grow. The soil was moist and healthy, and it was in a nine-inch, white pot with an aluminum dish underneath. After a year or two I was sure that it needed to be repotted but that was an endeavor well beyond my plant abilities. I was afraid of touching the leaves because I was sure the oil from my hands would ruin it. I was never sure what kind of soil to use in the new pot. And so I left it untouched.

Over time, the young growth had nowhere to go, so it died. The central stalk opened up and new growth came out from within it. The plant began to look completely different except for the fact that there were always new baby stalks popping up underneath, waiting for room to grow.

I could repot it to a larger pot. Maybe it would stay the same, just bigger. But since I still didn't feel comfortable repotting it, I would continue to watch it grow by way of change. Growth was happening. Growth was changing the nature of the plant.

I preferred plants that needed less change or plants that would simply grow like a vine, longer and longer. My most successful plant was from a clipping I made from one of Dan's plants. Its leaves were thick and green and oval. It took root in a plastic 14-inch pot. And it grew. And grew. I could mostly forget about it, maybe water it each week. This was my kind of plant. I was its kind of caregiver.

But most plants require both intuition and courage that I didn't have. I had one plant that seemed to be growing mold. I trimmed it and sent it affirmation; its vines withered leaving a few new, tiny little sprouts in a pot that was now way too big for it. I didn't know what to do so I left it there and I forgot about it for a bit. I wasn't angry or disappointed. I just thought that maybe it needed a little bit of time alone. Maybe it needed to decide what it wanted to be. And after ignoring it for awhile, it began to grow. The leaves turned a rich color of young green. It's as if the plant shed what is had been in order to become what it was to be.

Am I anthropomorphizing the plant? Of course I am. I do that.

I was told everyone can grow spider plants. It turns out that I can't. I thought we were doing fine until its leaves began to die and it was looking stringy. I looked it up online and I found the courage to repot my first plant. When I pulled it out of its pot, I discovered that its roots had grown round and round the pot; they were a knotted mess. The roots were taking up the bulk of the pot, leaving little room for the plant.

I unraveled its roots and found each tiny new baby. I separated them into three different pots. But this experience proved traumatic. None of them were doing well. I moved one outside thinking it might be a good change of scenery for it. But then I forgot about it. By the time I remembered it was out there, the leaves were light brown and limp. The soil was dry as—dirt. I decided to water it anyway. After two days, some of the leaves had turned green! It was a miracle! Some of the leaves were even standing straight up; they had bounced back. Why did they do that? How did they do that? Where did this plant get its resilience?

Why all the talk of plants? Well, I was told early in my ministry career that every pastor needs to have a garden or needs to keep plants because we learn so much about the human condition and about human growth when we tend to plants. I suppose that was good advice. And I have tried to learn a great deal about life by reflecting on how plants gro, or wither or die.

Sometimes people grow and need a new proverbial pot, a larger, more expansive environment. Sometimes people wither and look like they're going to die but with the right treatment and/or love they come back to life. Sometimes people shed lives just like a plant sheds leaves, messy dead stuff pooled all around the roots. But with compassion and/or help, people are able to trim off or clear out that which no longer serves them and in so doing, they will begin to thrive again. Sometimes people need to be watered (which I interpret as encouraged) weekly. Sometimes that much encouragement will only make them wet and moldy (which I interpret as lethargic and narcissistic). Growth is happening all the time. Growth was happening in me. Growth was happening in Pete. Growth was happening in my congregation. We were all very industrious. Sometimes visible, sometimes not. Life was all very resilient.

When it was all said and done though—I tend to do better with people than plants.

VULNERABLE UNDERSIDES

JOE, MY YOUNGEST STEPSON, HAD TWO CATS, brothers that he found in the woods. He treated them like people, loved them as part of our family, spoiled them like children. As a result, they were trusting. How did I know that? They didn't protect their bellies. Instead, even in front of strangers, they would stretch out, revealing their vulnerable underside. Only a well-loved animal trusts enough to expose his or her belly in this way.

So it is with cats, so it is with people. We don't let just anybody touch our bellies. And the inverse is true: We don't touch just anybody's bellies. When Pete greeted the boys he patted their belly. When Dan hugs his daughter, he pats her belly. When I hug both of them, I snake one arm around their back and with the other, I lightly place my hand on their belly. I don't pat, I just feel them as if acknowledging their presence.

The area around our belly button is sacred. Our "guts" inform our feelings. Our "guts" know things. Our "guts" have their own reactions. We were once connected to another human being through our belly button...through our Bee Bo!

Julia's favorite book at one time was Sandra Boynton's, *Belly Button Book.*

> "You might not know what BEE BO! means.
> Or maybe you've forgotten.
> It's just the tiny hippo way of saying...
> BELLY BUTTON!...
> BEE BO!"[4]

Any natural tendency we may have had to hide our belly buttons had been thwarted with Julia's love of this book. She

---

[4] Boynton, Sandra. *Belly Button Book,* Workman Publishing Company, 2005.

liked our belly buttons and if she caught a glimpse, she giggled and pointed and tried to muster the word "Bee Bo!" She discovered that everyone has one. Everyone has a belly button. Everyone has a vulnerable layer of skin protecting our insides. We don't let just anybody touch our vulnerable underside— neither the physical part of us that is vulnerable nor the emotional part that is vulnerable.

So often Pete didn't have a choice to withhold his vulnerability. Physicians poked and prodded him; friends and strangers asked him personal questions about his health. People talked about him as if he wasn't there. People watched him walk across the room, waiting for him to trip or fall but only to avert their eyes as if they didn't see him at all. Pete was wearing his vulnerability on the outside for everyone to see. And no one was comfortable with it. And so it seemed as though people put extra protection around themselves as they caught a glimpse of Pete's bared vulnerability.

A few years into Pete's diagnosis we were still learning about how his symptoms came and went. We were trying to get a handle on how much sleep he needed in order to keep his fatigue from overtaking his ability to move his legs. But our ability to monitor his symptoms was never going to be an algorithmic endeavor. Multiple sclerosis was way too capricious. He never knew what kind of energy a new day would bring. I remember one year during the week between Christmas and New Year that was filled with family and fun and friends and stress and food and wine. The week was ending with a church potluck. Pete needed help moving his legs into the car. I called Dan, my oldest stepson, and asked him to meet us at the house where together we carried Pete from the kitchen to the couch where Pete could take a nap. I believed his legs would bounce back after a little rest. I told Dan to go on home; if we needed anything I would call later.

I walked out with Dan and as soon as he got through the garage door, he began to cry. I tried to "catch" him as he apologized for his vulnerability of crying. I held him tightly as his arms were lodged between us as if protecting his belly. Or maybe he was protecting mine. I wasn't sure. The scene was ironic. His dad was so overtly vulnerable, so exposed. And while helping his dad in this physically vulnerable state, Dan's emotions began to show, revealing his own vulnerability. He tried to hide it. He did hide it from his dad but not from me. I was honored to have witnessed it. I was feeling vulnerable all the time, all the while trying to hide it from everyone else, particularly Pete. How horrible really, for us to hide our vulnerability just because we could, from the one who didn't have the option to hide his vulnerability.

After a bit Pete was still unable to move his legs. Joe had returned from a holiday gathering of his own, and I called Dan to come back home to help. We were going to have to carry him up 14 steps to a landing and then one more step off to the left. Together they created a gurney with a blanket. Joe grabbed Pete under his arms and Dan had his knees. They made it to the landing and rested for a bit. Joe sat down with Pete basically in his lap, with his arms wrapped around him. Dan rested his dad's legs and reached to adjust his dad's shirt that was exposing his belly. It was then that Pete touched his middle and said, "Bee Bo!"

As we chuckled, I was captivated by the long history of love that these three men had shared. While Pete's illness was awkward and frightening at times, Pete was teaching us to show our vulnerable undersides to one another. None of us liked it and we wouldn't choose this for ourselves or for one another. But indeed there was trust. And we only expose our vulnerable undersides to people we trust.

WHERE IS GOD
WHEN WE HURT?

A COUPLE IN MY CONGREGATION ASKED if I would come over for lunch to talk. So, one midweek afternoon, I ate vegetable pizza and drank soda while they told me about abuse that had happened in their family at the hands of a former priest. We also talked about family and friends who had come and gone from his life. We talked about their experience with job loss and debt. At some point they asked me point blank, "Where is God when we hurt?" Of course, they kept talking and so there was no space for me to attempt an answer. They kept talking and I kept listening. Above all else, pastors are professional listeners.

Their pain was real. Their story was incredibly vulnerable. And I knew I was one of the rare ones to have heard this story. At some point they even indicated they weren't sure that talking about it was going to do any good. The part that struck me was how they had clung to faith in God. The more I listened, the more I wondered if their question was less about where is God or where was God and more about, "Is it ok that I still believe in God even if God didn't protect me?"

I was having lunch with faith, rock-solid faith. Faith that says "I have no idea how this works but we will trust in something bigger and greater and more mysterious than we can comprehend." And now they had invited the pastor into the kitchen. This faith was dancing around or dancing on the question of whether or not God was or is or will be. I think it scared the shit out of all of us.

Of course, I didn't have an answer for any of this. A good friend of mine likes to say, "Faith is having no clue but having a lot of hope." I didn't have a clue what to say. If there really was a

God, then it didn't matter whether we held on or let go of our faith. God did not need us to cling so strongly to what we thought or hoped. We didn't have to hold tight to what we were told as children. I mean truly, if there was a God, then certainly God could function without any of us believing in God.

What I wanted to say during lunch was that the question was less about where God was when they were hurt and more about where the hell people were when horrible, painful things happened? After all, hurt people hurt other people. We live in a world filled with hurt people who are continually hurting other people. And all of us are going to at some point or another get caught in the crossfire of physical and emotional violence.

When they finally finished talking, they poured more soda for me. They both said they felt lighter just telling me the story. I hoped that was true. I, on the other hand, did not feel lighter. Instead, I had collected yet another story of trauma. I knew two more people who were trying to hold onto faith as a way of protecting themselves from more hurt. I gave them each a hug and pulled out of their driveway with a heavier heart.

WEEPING LEGS

A MAN IN MY CONGREGATION WAS FIGHTING CANCER, and his last round of chemo sent him to the hospital. His wife, his caregiver, visited each day, tried to keep doctors and medications straight. She watched like a hawk, asked questions, managed his needs as they emerged, and when she finally left for the day, she thought of all the things she didn't understand or didn't think to ask. Being a caregiver was exhausting—and no matter how much energy, critical thinking, serving, and loving we did, it was never finished.

One day I offered to stay at the hospital with him so she could go home and rest. His cancer had started in his throat four years earlier. He had "beaten" it with chemo that had burned the skin off his chest, ate away 80 pounds of him, and stripped all the hair from his head and his face. He had been a big, burly man. Not a lot of hair on his head, but a thick salt and pepper beard and mustache that served to hide his smirk. Without the facial hair, we discovered his mouth was actually kind of crooked. Yet it served up his North Jersey accent beautifully: less "fuhgeddaboudit" and more "ya-killin-me."

His throat cancer came back with a vengeance, moving to his liver and then his bones. He was in constant pain. I suppose he could've requested more pain medication, but he wanted to be aware of his surroundings, to be able to interact with others, to text his daughter, or to watch a tennis match on television. In my experience with various chronic illnesses, cancer is a different kind of fight. cancer doctors are a different kind of fighter as well. They wage war on cancer; their arsenals are filled with various poisons. Cancer doctors and treatments are like armies and artillery, each working on one section of the enemy named cancer. Cancer doctors beat down the enemy but never eradicate it. In fact that's true about cancer in general. We all have possible

WHO IS GOD WHEN WE HURT? 119

rogue cells that could become cancer. It's not an eradicated disease. It's a disease that we fight. I was sitting with a man who has fought and in so doing was so damaged, so tired, so diseased that he didn't have any fight left.

Every cancer story is different. But this story was about one man who spent the last of his energy fighting. When he was in the middle of fighting cancer, there was no room for talk of acceptance. I would say there was also very little room for vulnerability. Crying was acceptable at times and in small increments, but the majority of energy was reserved for the fight. Every day he woke up his strongest self, got out of bed swinging. There was no space reserved for reflection about this enemy, cancer, that was growing and breeding, mooching off of life as we knew it. There was a war going on—doctor as commander, patient as soldier, chemo as artillery and cancer as the enemy. My friend and congregant lay in a hospital bed; his body was a war-torn battlefield.

And so I pulled my chair up next to this battlefield. I was drinking coffee; he was eating oatmeal. He was on his second bowl actually. His son had told me that his dad was eating oatmeal like a small child—loads of sugar and lots of milk. It's the only thing that his stomach enjoyed, and so the hospital happily served him bowl after bowl. At one point he looked up at me with his crooked smile and said, "I love this oatmeal." I choked on my coffee laughing at him.

He laughed, too, and followed it with a wink of sorts. I'd known this man for years. A laugh and a wink. I was gonna miss them both. I took a deep breath and began an uncomfortable conversation with the question, "Do you want to talk about your funeral?"

He did. In fact, he had already picked out songs. He wanted me to create an environment where people knew God was with them and where they could be challenged to live fully. Through this conversation, we determined to have his funeral in the church rather than at a funeral home. If he wanted songs and spiritual challenges, a sanctuary seemed better suited. He finished his oatmeal and I told him that I had enough information to honor his wishes. Then we held silence together. I wanted to say something, anything. But I was holding back tears too hard to speak. Finally, I was able to muster the words, "This sucks." Tears streamed down my face. He replied, "Yeah, it does." Tears streamed down his face too.

I moved closer to him so that we could hug. Beside a hospital bed, underneath florescent lights, with tubes that tethered him to medicine, and the sounds of beeping from across the hall, we hugged and we wept. Our embrace was eventually broken up by the need for tissues. I found them; they were beside a stack of clean, absorbent pads, like the ones that were underneath his legs.

I noticed that water had begun to pool by his legs. His legs were flushed red and filled with fluid. His body could no longer process fluids so his skin was serving as an escape valve. The pool of water beneath his legs was the fluid leaking through his pores. I asked if I could lift his legs and change the pad underneath them. He said, "Yeah, but my legs hurt a lot to be touched." I nodded and said, "Ok, I'll be careful and if it's too much we'll call a nurse." I knelt beside his legs and looked up at him with a slight smile and said, "Are you ready?" He nodded. I reached for his rash-filled legs putting one hand under his ankle and the other closer to his knee. With tears in my eyes, I lifted his legs and water wept from them.

When I interned as a chaplain, we were told (in strict terms) not to provide physical care for patients. There were other professionals who did the physical work of caring for someone. We provided pastoral care, not physical care. But when you became someone's pastor, when you begin to love specific people, physical, emotional, and spiritual care don't have clear boundaries. Physical care communicates emotional care. Emotional care lends itself to spiritual conversations. Spiritual conversations help us care for one another physically. And perhaps more honestly, physical care, emotional care, and spiritual care don't come in the same order every time.

After we cleaned up his weeping legs, after we dried our tear-filled eyes, I headed to the elevator to go home. And as the door closed, I thought, "We had just started to say goodbye."

Startled, I Wake

STARTLED, I WAKE;
scared is my instinct.
My mental faculties
upright,
readied with reason
fast to respond.

He's on the floor,
lodged between the bed and the
motorized wheelchair,
a gift that has kept his falling to a minimum.
"You won't fall if you're sitting down,"
said his neurologist.

He can't feel his legs,
he doesn't have to tell me.
They lie there, unmoving,
slightly less colorful.

I reach for him,
holding his hands and propping him upright.
He says, "I feel blood."
I turn on the lights.
I have not put my glasses on;
I can't see anything.

OK, I say. We'll check it out.
First, let's get up onto the bed again.
"I was going to the bathroom."
OK, we'll figure that out too.
Bend legs first,

Lift to kneeling position.
"Can you do this with me?"
Yes, I think so.
Up to stand, quickly twist
we sit on the edge of the bed.

When we fell asleep, he was so tired.
Beyond tired. Yet his body was
buzzing.
His energy shaking the bed,
I could feel it once I settled myself.
Now he is calm.
Still tired, but not
buzzing.

Now he is tearful, dreading his dependence
I look for the source of blood.
A gouge to his head – but once cleaned up
more like a cut.
A scrape on his arm,
a ding to his ankle – at least it's a different ankle.
The other is still healing.
His legs – they're discolored – and
they alarm me.

Clean wounds, we crawl
under the covers together.
Touching, soothing one another.
He falls asleep first.
I turn on Twitter and fill a glass of water.

Two hours later, he wakes me.
I am not startled this time.
My mental faculties
upright,
readied with grace
fast with mercy.

Again, we crawl
under the covers together.
Touching, soothing one another.
We both fall asleep.

And it is the morning after.
Awakened by my cell phone
ringing in the other room.
Two cups of coffee and breakfast,
I am upright.
Hoping he will sleep most of the day.
Yet I listen for him to wake.

Caregiving

WHAT DOES THAT MEAN? I MEAN REALLY – WHAT DOES IT MEAN?
I give care?
Like a present on a birthday. Here you go,
open it—it's "care." I care.
No need to say what I care about. It may not even be you.
I care. In other words, I don't not care.

A friend of mine has a 10-year-old who told her, "Well, Mom,
you don't care anyway."
What?! What do you mean I don't care?
Well, Mom—you always say—"go ahead, I don't care."
No. That's not what that means.
Of course I care, she said.
But his reasoning was sound.
She had said—often—I don't care.
Can I go to the neighbor's to play? I don't care.
What do you want for dinner? I don't care.
Mom, can I bring this to school? I don't care.
What should I have for a snack? I don't care.
Coke or Pepsi? I don't care.

And yet here is a gift, wrapped for you in colorful pastels.
There is no bow
however.
I couldn't find a bow.
And no need for a card because I didn't think you would care.
Go ahead—open it. And as I smile watching you
you rip at the colors to find a box of "care."
Thank you. You care.
Yes, I do.
No, it is not that.

Caregiving.
What does that mean? I mean really—what does it mean?
I give care?
I give care, offering it like my weekly offering
in church. The plate is passed and I reach into my wallet, leafing
through to find that there is indeed care in a careless society. I
count out an appropriate amount and fold it as to hide my
amount of giving.
When the plate is passed, I avert my eyes to the usher
but smile nonetheless when I give my care, grasping the plate
and pass it to my left,
again averting my eyes yet smiling.

I look down at my knees and then come back to reality
the piano is playing a haunting tune. Why haunting?
Why play something haunting while we are giving our cares?
Unless the music is taking them away.
I cast all my cares upon you.
I lay all of my burdens down at your feet.
And anytime I don't know what to do,
I will cast all my cares upon you.

Caregiving, carecasting...

Ah... it means casting care like a fly fisherman. A
long line with colorful plastic feathers at one end, attached to a
hook. Switch, switch, switch—the line floats over head
and with the flick of my wrist, I cast—switch.
The feathery hook barely touches the water—luring
the fish to the surface with one question, "What was that?"
Looks like lunch.
Casting care. Care giving.
A rhythmic flow of the thin, barely noticeable line
moving to and fro—arching and falling
like a giant bubble, like the ones we hope to create
while playing outside with our children.
Blowing bubbles, casting lines,

casting care,
caregiving.

Small blue plastic container labeled "bubble magic."
Complete with a
tiny plastic magnifying glass.
Lift it out to discover it is
not made of glass at all—it is filled with soap.
Soap that when blown lightly will make bubbles.
Lots of tiny bubbles.
Sometimes streams of them. Sometimes
one big large one—if blown with patience and an intentional

stream of constant air pressure,
the same pressure, the
right pressure—don't stop, if you do it will pop.
The bubble is growing and growing and
growing and then it pops.
Dip again, try again. Bubbles, lots of tiny bubbles.
All around, go collect them, catch them. Watch them
wash your arms and legs,
one round spot at a time.

Blowing bubbles,
Casting Care.
Care Giving.
I care.
I cast.
I patiently, intentionally

attempt big bubbles.
Slowly, slowly, with consistent pressure.
Until it pops. It always pops.
Dip again, try again.

To Help or Not to Help, Part One

IT'S 9 P.M. AND PETE ASKED ME TO HELP. He noticed blood on the kitchen floor and asked me to investigate where the blood had come from. He had scraped off a chunk of flesh from his right ankle. His sock was saturated with blood. "You didn't feel this?" I asked. "No," he said. I took a deep breath as I headed to the kitchen to start cleaning up the mess. On my way, my internal monologue started.

You've been concerned about his feet for a while now. Ever since he started using the wheelchair, his feet look bluish and puffy. You need to pay more attention. Like you need to pay attention to how his right leg has been weaker than his left. And he has lost dexterity in his fingers, too. And his balance…his core muscles have started to show signs of fatigue.

As I dropped to my knees with a wet towel and some soap, the internal monologue turned to an internal holler for help. "Help! Someone help me!" I knew I was in over my head. Like I've said before, no one carries the pressure and weightiness of chronic illness more than the caregiver. No one. Life was getting heavier and heavier and I felt as though I had reached my limit. I just couldn't pick it all up anymore.

The cry for help continued only inside of me, drifting from my head to my heart and back again. I cleaned his ankle and then the floor. I cleaned the blood that had dripped across the carpet. And when I thought I was done, I found blood on the leg rests of his wheelchair. Yuck. Gross. Then his ankle started bleeding again. So I was stooped down cleaning up his ankle for the second time when I came to my senses and said, "Wait a minute, Pete you can do this."

He was able to elevate his leg; he was able to clean it

himself. Maybe he couldn't scrub the rug on his hands and knees but he was still able to take care of his own ankle. And yet he was relying on me or I was enabling him to rely on me. So I stood up in the middle of our gigantic handicap accessible bathroom sticking up for myself and my time and my energy. Like an attorney, I argued on behalf of the spouse who is being taken over by the role of caregiver. "Which do you want?" I asked, "a spouse or caregiver?"

With Neosporin in one hand and Band-Aids in the other, I asked my beloved, "Which do you want?"

The answer was both. Well, he wanted a spouse but needed a caregiver. And he would prefer the caregiver also be me, his spouse and his beloved.

The next morning I heard the beep of his motorized wheelchair come on. The sounds of the wheelchair were the background soundtrack to our lives. The wheelchair woke up with "budup." It was 5:44 a.m. After the wheelchair spoke, I heard Pete: A tiny grunt as he swung his legs out of bed, hoping that the momentum would position him upright. Then I heard another grunt or two as he transferred from bed to chair. Then the wheelchair was on the move. It made the sound "shoo" as it slid across the carpet until it finally stopped with an "oop."

I lay there waiting to worry. I was going to wait five minutes until I started to wonder about the silence I was hearing. But then those five minutes were up, so I gave it another five. If there was another five minutes of silence I was going to ask, "You ok?" Usually that was followed by "Yup." Usually means 90% of the time. But 10% of the time, the answer was, "No, I could use some help." This time it was the 10%.

The same ankle wound was open. Clean the wound. Clean the floor. Neosporin. Band-Aids.

This time there were no questions about whether he wanted a caregiver or a spouse. We had already determined the answer was both. I was a spouse/caregiver. The hardest task was not just balancing those roles but parsing which was needed when. When Pete first cut his ankle, it was 9 p.m. We were at the end of a full week of work and play—a big party, an early morning with our granddaughter, a movie, and a meeting with a builder. He was exhausted. I was, too.

The issue I had with helping Pete do something that he could do himself earlier no longer applied in the middle of the night. The next morning was Sunday. I really wanted him to be able to get to church. Church was where our friends were. Church was where our support was. Church was the place where everyone knew his name. It was the place where he gave and received love. If he missed church, I might be the only human contact he had that week.

Help! Somebody help me!

When 8:30 a.m. rolled around, Pete was too tired to join me at church. Everyone asked how they could help Pete. Nobody asked how they could help me. But then again, I hadn't asked for help yet.

To Help or Not to Help, Part Two

"PETE, CAN I HELP YOU WITH THAT?"

"Hey, you need some help?"

"Honey, what can I do?"

Over time I had grown accustomed to asking some form of the question "Can I help you?" more than a dozen times each day. The idea, the possibility, the potential of me being needed to help Pete loomed over me. More and more, Pete needed help with everyday tasks. His hands were shakier; his feet were less sturdy. Lifting a pot of coffee and pouring coffee into a mug required a certain steadiness. Walking or wheeling across the kitchen and into the living room with said cup of coffee required sturdiness. Putting dishes in the dishwasher, putting clothes away, lifting the laundry basket—he often needed help. But asking if he needed help over and over throughout the day was frustrating me.

It wasn't just asking. It was that I asked and then I would have to wait for an answer. No response. I waited. I watched. I took mental notes. I noticed his shakiness or sturdiness or lack thereof. I assessed whether I should intervene without invitation or continue to wait for a response. I often waited for a response, allowing him to keep his autonomy, let him do for himself. But then eventually, I would ask again. This time I would add information I had gathered while watching, "Honey, it looks like you could use some help. What can I do?"

"Nothing. I'm fine," he said.

Right. Shaking my head and thinking to myself, "No you're not. You're shaky and unsteady."

And the silence that lingered between us, which only I felt was breeding frustration. My internal monologue would fill in the silence by creating a loop of questions and comments to myself— *Why won't he let me help him? It looks so hard to do it his way. Why does he insist on doing everything his way and by himself? He's not fine. He's got MS. He could hurt himself. He could fall.* Eventually, I couldn't keep my thoughts to myself, I'd say, "You know if you fall, it's a lot harder for me to help you then."

He replied, "I'm not going to fall." I'd add, "Yes, but sometimes you do."

Again with the silence.

I kept watching. Silently. Whatever I was doing beforehand had completely gone by the wayside. I stopped living my life and I was watching his life. I had become a bystander in Pete's life, waiting for my cue to enter the scene. And the horrible truth here was that most of the time—90% of the time—he did just fine without my help. He gets coffee by himself. He goes to the bathroom by himself. He puts his clothes away or put the dishes in the dishwasher without my help. My own anxiety level was the problem, not Pete's level of ability. So one day we made a deal.

I agreed to stop asking Pete if I can help and Pete promised to ask for help when he needed it.

Two days later our deal was tested.

Pete came out of the bathroom, headed to bed and fell. His leg didn't get the communication from his brain and his body crumbled slowly to the floor. His falls were less like tripping and more like sinking to the floor. And so Pete was sitting on his ankles 15 feet from the bed. His teeth were brushed, his medication taken, he was ready for sleep. I, too was ready for sleep. I was in bed, book in my lap, glass of water at my bedside table. I saw this happen out of the corner of my eye. I took a deep breath. And then I did the unthinkable. I turned my head so that I could not see him. It was the only way I could keep my part of the deal. I felt callous and uncaring. I thought I was the worst partner ever to live on the face of the earth. What kind of person doesn't ask if she can help?

But we made a deal.

I didn't offer help. And Pete didn't ask for help. I kept

reading my book and Pete made his way to bed. Without my help. Once he was settled I looked over at him. Before I could say anything, he asked, "How was that?"

"Really hard," I said.

Emotional Inventory

My patience has run thin.
Like green, wrinkly tissue paper left over from Christmas
I'm using it to wrap
a re-gifted present.

My anxiety has run away.
Like a vibrating washing machine that's stuck on spin
I wait for clean towels
so I can take a shower.

My want has arrived.
Like a ringing telephone that wakes me dead sleeping
I reach to answer it
without recognizing the number.

My mistrust has taken up residence.
Like a squirrel stealing birdseed while the birds nap at noontime,
I'm waiting for anyone
to correct such injustice.

My trust in God has disappeared.
Like a prayer that rolled down the hill,
I've tossed the good
out to the curb.

My love may have no chance.
Like a sadness has eaten my faith as a snack
I'm holding out for hope
to be served for lunch.

OVERACTIVE GRIEF

WE WENT OUT TO DINNER ONE NIGHT—movies, dinner and even ice cream with a little coffee house music.

By the end of the night I was disgusted by almost everything Pete did. The way he put his coat on or had a hard time putting his coat on. The way I had to secure his wheelchair in the van. The fact that there were no van-accessible handicap spots in the parking lot. So we parked far away where we could find two adjacent spots. And when we had to leave, the parking lot was full. So we pulled out, set the ramp down. And of course where we pulled out, there were two other cars trying to leave.

When we left the theater, although I was walking with him and held the door for him, a stranger assumed that Pete was alone. And then acknowledged me, "Oh you're with this young woman." I was tired of being the young woman with the chronically ill, disheveled-looking man who needed a haircut and a shirt that fit him.

I was tired of having to think about Pete's well-being all the time, his meals, his clothing, his access, his social life. No one was thinking about me except me. I wanted this date, so I arranged it. I had wanted a night out with him, so I planned it. I wanted something that seemed normal. But nothing was normal.

Normal was something that used to happen. Normal was partnership. Normal was when my partner helped carry stuff from the car into the house. Normal was when my partner, my closest friend, brought me coffee or tea in the morning or took a walk with me at the end of the day. (OK, the coffee thing was real but we never took a walk at the end of the day.) Normal was having my companion carry a level of responsibility for our lives. Nothing was going to be normal because our partnership was lopsided. I was carrying more of the partnership and it was wearing me down.

For a while Pete saw an acupuncturist where the receptionist also had MS. The two of them used to talk about a "normal" day. She had cleverly named her MS. Using MS as initials, she called her disease "Martha," short for Martha Stewart. Pete really liked this idea. He started calling his "Bill Gates." When we arrived at the acupuncturist, he always asked her, "How's Martha doing today?" She responded often with something like, "Oh she woke up on the wrong side of the bed today. And how about you? How's ol' Bill doing for you?" One time he shrugged and said, "I haven't thought of him today." Objectifying the illness and giving it a life of its own, because multiple sclerosis does have a life of its own, was really helpful for me to see that all of this analyzing Pete's well-being was not helpful. It was adding to my stress level, pushing my grief button unnecessarily, and ultimately taking away my life. Each day was whatever it was going to be. And that somehow was "normal" for them.

Pete was able to accept the new normal better than I was. When people questioned how he was able to accept the ups and downs of every day, he said, "You know, no one knows what kind of day they're going to have. We all wake up and get what we get. I just happen to have some unique things I wake up with. Each day is going to be what it's going to be."

I tried to talk to Pete about how badly I was doing. The conversation went like this: I used 500 words and he used six. I tried again with another 500 words. He responded with these four "What do you want?" I answered him. I said, "I want my partner back."

I was losing my partner. And I missed him.

It was horrible to miss someone who I saw all the time. In fact, I saw him more at this point in our marriage than I ever did. Since he was approved for federal disability, he was home all the time. We were adjusting, like how retired couples have to adjust to seeing each other more. The adjustment was harder than we thought it would be.

I had always had a job where I worked a little from home but now my home had activity in it. The television was on; music was on. I couldn't work the same way I once had. And since

Pete's presence was less partnership and more duty, I had started to hope that he was sleeping when I got home so that I could rest. I was embarrassed to feel this way. I felt guilty for being weary from this unwanted journey with multiple sclerosis. But when I came home to a quiet house, when Pete was asleep, I cried more and more. I started to wonder if I was depressed.

It felt like my grief button had started to malfunction. I have started to think we only have one grief button. When someone dies, our grief button gets pushed. When someone is diagnosed with multiple sclerosis, our grief button is pushed. When we have plans to do something and they fall through, our grief button is pushed. When we spill milk, our grief button is pushed. We had experienced so many little losses that my grief button was overused. I started to think it was malfunctioning.

For several years, Pete and I had been living on high alert. We were always watching and waiting for something to happen with his health. We waited and when faced with a problem, we evaluated, dissected, analyzed and responded the best we could. And then we set ourselves on high alert again, waiting for the next thing to happen.

The constant analysis was exhausting and discouraging. Whenever Pete woke with less energy, I asked myself, what made this day different than other days? Why was he more fatigued? Was it something he ate? Was it environmental? What could either of us do to help his fatigue level? How would I ever adjust to a new normal if every day was unpredictable? I didn't want to adjust to an unpredictable, uber-analytical, anxious, depressing life. It was time to consider pharmacological help.

My therapist and I decided to consult with my primary care physician about medication. Our primary care physician had been with us through this entire journey. She was the one who first ordered a CT scan and the first to confirm the "nonspecific white matter" on the MRI. She helped us find our first neurologist; I trusted her. I was able to cry in front of her. She trusted me as a caregiver. She listened to me as a person. She cared about my health as much as she cared for Pete's health.

I sat in the exam room, down the hallway on the right. I worried that she would disagree with me and I would be left with what I had begun to call overactive grief. And then I worried she would agree. What if I was mentally ill? Mentally unstable? What if I was correct and my brain had been damaged along the way.

She agreed that I was experiencing situational depression and anxiety. And I exhaled. I left the office with a prescription for a medication that works on both my combination of depression and anxiety.

I continued to see my therapist after I began taking medication. I was grateful for the clarity that came with the medication. I wanted to understand myself. With the help of my therapist, I discovered how much my life had changed. This trauma had jostled me and the pieces didn't end up in the same place. This encounter with multiple sclerosis had changed me. I was not going to be the same person as before diagnosis, nor would I react to myself or anyone else the same as before diagnosis.

I can only speak to my experience. I had situational depression that stemmed from a traumatic experience, namely the diagnosis of a chronic illness. The constant changes and losses created an anxiety loop and I was not able to get it to stop with sheer willpower. My personal experience with medication was easy. The first prescription worked for me. But as a pastor, I have witnessed many situations where diagnosing, treating and living with mental illness was much harder. I estimate that 20% of my congregation is actively treating a mental illness through therapy and/or medication. I believe another 10% is actively avoiding their mental health. I imagine there is yet another 10% who are struggling but have not yet named it as a mental health issue. For me, a combination of medication and talk therapy worked.

Pete agreed. A little less than two weeks later I sheepishly asked Pete if he saw any difference in my emotional well-being. He did not hesitate with these words "You are a different person." I knew he was right. All of those irritations were still there but they weren't so edgy, so sensitive, so overwhelming.

Medication allowed my brain to stop with spinning for answers and grabbing for control of my life. My emotions had been on a roller coaster ride that never stopped. I was grieving each loss, up and down, up and down. I was bracing for impact and then no impact would happen. I was adjusting my life and it didn't make any difference.

When I took medication, my grief button got a reprieve. It began to heal, or something like heal. It's almost as if it adjusted to the new way it would be pushed. I began to have perspective and patience with myself, with Pete and with the unpredictability of multiple sclerosis.

Once, however, I let my prescription run out. It was not because I was irresponsible. I had asked Pete to renew the prescription for me. He did. But two days before I was to run out, it had not arrived and after calling the mail-order drug company, I found they had not been able to reach my physician . I made three calls to my physician's office; they never called me back. In the meantime I ran out of drugs and I began to feel the stress, anxiety, and pain of being a caregiver again. I forgot what the anxiety and worry had been like. I had forgotten about crying all the time. I had forgotten about feeling so out of control of my emotions. I was now face to face with emotional instability because I had the perspective of what emotional stability felt like. I was uncomfortable with myself. With my tears. With my panic. I was anxious and depressed again.

In the earlier years of Pete's diagnosis, when I cried all the time, when my anxiety was palpable, loved ones used to ask if I was seeing a therapist, or if I had considered medication to help me through my grief. I knew they were asking out of love for me but they were also asking because they were uncomfortable with my grief, with my emotional instability. Mental illness is uncomfortable, not just for the one suffering from it. For those in relationship with those suffering from it, it's downright difficult.

Before medication, when I was trying my best with talk therapy and exercise and meditation and prayer and good nutrition, I could see how others around me simply wanted things to be more manageable for me. And if things could be easier for me, they would be easier for them as they were in relationship with me. Pete's illness was uncomfortable for him and for those around him. My emotions were uncomfortable for me and for those around me. We had no way to control what was happening to him. Multiple sclerosis comes at us at its own pace, in its own way. It doesn't ask permission and it doesn't yield.

We were going to continue to experience loss. My grief button would continue to be pushed. I was grateful for the help of medication to manage my malfunctioning grief button.

STRESS, GRIEF, AND HORMONES

IN ADDITION TO MY EMOTIONS AND THE MEDICATION that helped manage those emotions, I felt my hormones played a big role in my stability. The bloating, the aching lower back, the cramping and, of course, the messiness of women's menstruation were not a welcome reality in the world of men. In order to make it in our world, women have had to hide, alter, control, or subdue this very natural, beautiful, miraculous monthly occurrence. We spend more time discussing how to overcome it than we do talking about what it does to us. Collectively, we spend a fortune on making it not affect us and our lifestyle. A rough estimate says that I've taken 4500 Advil caplets, my muscle relaxer of choice. Those 4500 caplets have given me an esophageal problem. But I'd take them again because taking those pills made it possible for me to attend school, go to work, and participate in my daily life without pain.

I noticed that my hormones played a role in my anger and irritability. I started to track my emotional outbursts because being unreasonable is not something I wanted to be and not something that works in a work environment or play environment or friend environment or it turns out, being unreasonable wasn't good for my marriage.

There was almost nothing worse than discovering that the reason I was unable to manage emotions was not solely because my grief button was malfunctioning but also because I was about to get my period! If I analyzed my data, I was rational for 28 days. I was happy, easygoing, reasonable, and otherwise fun to live with—for 28 days. And then whatever was actually unmanageable in my life cut through the normal barrier and asserted its opinion, usually with anger and irritability. For a long time I thought if I tracked my period I would be able to negotiate how and when that tornado hit. I couldn't. I was angry and frustrated and impatient with my life, primarily at home, and most specifically with my relationship with multiple sclerosis. I didn't want this relationship. For most of the month I was able to ignore the anger I felt about having to have a relationship with MS.

As I talked through the stress in my life with my therapist, my friends, and Pete, I started to take seriously this voice that cut through during my menstruation. This voice was not unreasonable. It spoke truth. I was under a lot of stress. And with the addition of multiple sclerosis and the changes in my marriage, I had reached a limit to how much stress I was able to take. For most of the month, I was able to "accept the things I could not change." But when my hormones fluctuated, this tornado picked me up by the scruff of the neck and tossed me around like I was a rabid cat.

Most of the month I could live with the anxiety of never knowing how a day was going to go. Most of the month I could subdue the growing number of stories I was collecting of people who were hurting. But what I was really doing was ignoring myself. By ignoring myself I wasn't living my life, I was avoiding it. My hormones—they were my truth tellers. My hormones provided the needed voice that said, "No more, Beth. You actually can't handle the stress you're under." My hormones were right. I was living with chronic stress. I experienced anxiety every time Pete moved. I woke at night when he woke and I kept one eye open as he went to the bathroom and didn't shut that eye until he was back in bed.

We were trying to fight MS and we were losing. We were out of our league. We felt outrun, outsmarted, outmatched. Since we couldn't win against MS we would often fight one another. I married someone very different than me. His differences were wonderfully attractive until something important or scary happened. When stress hit I didn't want to be partnered with someone so different from me; I wanted to be partnered with someone who understood me and who I understood. I wanted to be married to someone who processed and reasoned like me! But no, I married an alien; a calm, reasonable, level-headed, often slow to respond alien. Why wasn't he angry at the changes in our lives? Why wasn't he afraid that he might fall at any moment? Why didn't he show signs of coming undone?

Pete was making no sense to me and I was certainly making no sense to him. Inside I was hurting, and I desperately wanted someone to take my stress seriously. For 28 days of each month, I was able to ignore myself, my fear, my hurt. But for three to four days each month, my hormones spoke the truth and my fear yelled as loud as it could to get someone's attention. I needed to start listening.

FACING THE WRONG WAY

WHILE I WAS SUFFERING IN MY GRIEF AND struggling with my mental health, I had a dream.

I dreamed that I was in a church service, a Presbyterian church service, along a shoreline. The back of the church was open to the ocean. When I looked right, there was a semi-enclosed staircase. I began to climb and it was very steep at first but the more I climbed the rise of the steps changed. To the left was always the water but to the right there were different churches. I climbed and I climbed discovering Lutheran, Methodist, Baptist, Quaker, and what appeared to be Amish people gathered in prayer. And then I climbed some more until I saw a group of African people worshiping near an oasis. There was a font that looked like a birdbath. Two or three other women were gathered around the font. They were the first to invite me in, saying, "Stop climbing. Come touch the water." I did; I touched the water and I stayed a little while to rest. But the staircase called to me and I was sure that there was something better at the top.

I climbed another flight and a half where there were Catholics worshiping. The communion table was set with the Eucharist and candles. They, too, invited me saying, "Stop climbing. Come and eat. You're almost at the top, a few more steps and then a wonderful view of the water." I looked at them and then looked toward the steps. They continued, "The breeze will be refreshing, of course." I asked, "Are you sure that's all there is? The steps must lead to something else." I chose to continue rather than to stay and eat. I continued my journey upward.

Finally, I arrived at the top of the staircase. I emerged onto the roof of a large building. The shoreline still to my left was not the ocean but a vast sea. Before me was a sidewalk, maybe 30 feet and then I could see no more. To my right was the building that housed the many worship spaces and traditions I had seen. I looked to the sea but there was no way down to it; the staircase had led to the top of a steep wall overlooking the sea. I walked to the end of the sidewalk and found there too was a steep wall. Below in the distance were houses and other sidewalks. I turned around and looked at the staircase. I had come a long way!

I sat atop the wall, my feet dangling off the side. I tried to remember what I had seen on my climb when I was so determined to make it to the top. I remembered the occasional open windows along the staircase that provided me with fresh air. Of course, I remembered the Africans with their birdbath-baptismal font and the Catholics with their candles and their invitation to a meal. And then I thought I'd ask them what they thought of this staircase. I descended the few steps back to the Catholics and asked what they made of the staircase. What was its purpose? "To climb when needed," they said. I told them that I had come from the bottom, the very bottom. "Should I go back down?" I asked.

They asked, "Haven't you had enough climbing? Aren't you tired?" "Yes," I said. I was. I was so tired of climbing. So I rested with them by the candles and they fed me. But soon I felt the call to climb back down.

In no time I was passing the Africans with their font. Their presence felt familiar, like sisters. So I sat with them awhile, around the font. When I continued my descent, I began to slow down. I was interested in these others I had passed so quickly on my way up the stairs.

On my descent, I came across the Amish folks. They greeted me, looked me in the eye. Their own eyes smiled at me. They were busy making a meal. I felt welcomed to stay but wanted to find out what else was on my way back home. I wondered if they had climbed the stairs but I didn't ask.

I came to the Lutherans. There was a curtain between their space and the staircase. When I opened the curtain I was at their altar. There was a window that opened to the sea. I asked them about the staircase and they said they knew of the staircase but rarely did anyone climb it. Instead they could see the sea from their pews. They preferred to sit together and look out the window at the sea.

I paused at a strangely familiar sanctuary that I skipped altogether, perhaps one from my childhood or one from a movie. I didn't stop there because there weren't any people in it.

Then the steps became steep again. I had forgotten they were steeper at the beginning. The staircase became enclosed and very narrow; I had to hold on with both hands and descend backwards until I finally reached the floor. A hard concrete floor. Around the corner was the Presbyterian church. Their pews were facing away from the sea. And the back of the sanctuary was completely open. A patio led out to the shoreline. Why were they not facing the sea? I thought about taking my place with the others. After all, these were my people, right? And it appeared they were to start worship soon. But the sea was right there. I wanted to take a quick trip to the water before worship, and if I was honest, perhaps instead of worship. I stepped onto the patio and then onto the sand and then I woke.

LEAVING OUR HOUSE

WHEN I BECAME A SCIBIENSKI, I MOVED into Pete's house in Dunellen, New Jersey. Dan was in college; Joe was in middle school. Pete often described their world as one in which "they grunted in the morning to one another and where they never needed to put the toilet seat down." Even though I was a verbal processor and liked to talk over coffee, they allowed me to move in. They loved that house. I loved the house too. It was a small Cape Cod on a quiet street. Their home was strewn with memories, and it was safe. Once when I was dating Pete I came over after a really hard day at work and basically asked if I could just take a nap on his couch. He made me tea and brought me Entenmanns cinnamon mini-muffins. I stretched out and melted into their space.

When both of the guys had graduated high school, we set out to downsize. We purchased a townhome a couple of towns over. Although Pete and I were excited to have a home that was "ours" I knew it was really hard for the three of them to say goodbye to the home they loved. They had memories of falling in love, fighting with each other, playing with each other, eating chicken patties and "potato puffs" for dinner.

On moving day I was packing up the last box. I looked out my bedroom window and saw Pete, Dan, and Joe in the driveway hugging each other in a tight circle of love and understanding. I wondered if our new house would ever feel like home to them. It did. Joe came home here and there throughout college. They both brought friends, girlfriends, and strays over for dinner, always assuming that our home would welcome and feed whoever entered it. We made new memories as a family in this new house.

Dan moved all of his stuff back to our house when he moved to Ecuador for a year to teach English. Joe had come back to bury his cats while we were in this house. Dan had moved his pregnant wife, Faith, to our house while they were in between houses. Our granddaughter, Julia, came home from the hospital to our new house. We loved this house, but it was not great for someone with MS. There were steps everywhere. Up to the kitchen from the garage, up to the living room from the kitchen, a full flight to the bedrooms. Pete went from using a walking stick to a cane, a cane to a walker, a walker to a rollator in this house. There were assistive devices littered all over this house.

The real estate market had tanked and the idea of selling just seemed ridiculous. We would lose everything. We waited to see if it would get any better, and it just didn't rebound quickly enough. We cut our losses, sold our home, and looked for something to rent that fit our nonnegotiable needs: one floor, no steps, accessible bathrooms.

Pete qualified to live in a 55-plus community, so we assumed the accessibility would be better in an adult community. We found it wasn't. Handicap accessible doors are often an upgrade that people don't choose. And most people really do not understand that walkers and wheelchairs may be able to get into the front door but they most likely will not be able to get into the bathrooms. Bathroom doors, in particular, are thinner than other doors in homes. And then if the door was big enough to get a wheelchair into the home, there often was not enough room to close the door once the wheelchair was inside.

We found a place. A condo, two bedrooms, two baths, a little bit outside of our budget but it was beautiful, and it had everything we needed. And the kitchen was most likely the nicest kitchen I would ever have. We began to pack, to purge, to prepare for another adventure. In the attic, I discovered two boxes of the guys' stuff from their childhood.

I was happy to move the boxes to our new home but asked them to go through them. They found forgotten treasures, they laughed, they threw things out, and we were only left with one box of Joe's stuff and a Ouija board to move with us to our new home. Dan had taken or thrown out everything that was his. This was it. Once again, I wondered if they would feel comfortable enough to fall asleep on the couch in our new home. Probably yes. Would they continue to bring strays home? Probably yes to that, too.

This was a different move than the move to our townhome. Our townhome was creating a home for us as a couple, wanting to make sure our adult children felt welcome. This move was due to reasons out of our control. Multiple sclerosis was forcing us to move. This move was about facing our future rather than building our future. Right before the last box left, I sat on that spot by my closet door, the one where the rug had started to come up. I said "good bye" not just to a home but to a future that was derailed by MS. I tried to let go of what had not turned out how we thought it would.

THE SIMPLE ACT OF GETTING DRESSED, OR I HATE MS

"BETH, WHEN YOU HAVE A MOMENT, I need some help," Pete *calls from the bedroom.*

I was in the bathroom, just a few feet away. "Yep, coming."

"I can't lift my legs," he says.

The simple act of getting dressed—thwarted by multiple sclerosis.

Scratch that—sometimes getting dressed isn't a simple act.

Getting dressed is actually really hard. It requires an enormous amount of core strength and balance. Getting dressed uses our upper body and lower body. Try this: Sit on the couch, raise your hands, and lift your feet off the ground. Now hold that position for awhile. Core strength. Pete's core was starting to take a hit with the progression of his MS.

Pete had started to need help getting dressed maybe once a month. In the moment I was typically able to respond and help. One leg, then the other. Sometimes I held his middle and he pulled his pants up. Sometimes he stood and I pulled his pants up. We were still figuring out the best technique.

Pete's version of secondary progressive multiple sclerosis was very slow moving. Without question it had been a downward trajectory, but we had no idea the angle of the slope nor did we know what was going to happen next. No one could have told us that the next step would be needing help to get dressed. And I had no problem helping in this way, even with compassion and love. But afterward, I interrogated the hell out of the situation. I wanted to know why this was happening. Was it really part of the progression of MS or was it something else? Could we avoid this change in our lifestyle? Was it medication based, nutrition based, sleep based?

For example, one day we were supposed to have company over and Pete needed help getting dressed. While I was helping him get dressed, I thought that perhaps he was too tired to have company. If he needed help for this, he probably needed to sleep. And then I wondered if there was some other reason that he needed help. So, after we got Pete's pants on, before we were about to have company, I asked a series of questions. "What's going on? Why can't you feel your legs? When is your medicine due?" Then I found out one of his meds that gives him a little extra energy should have been taken a couple hours earlier. I freaked out saying, "Well, if *I* were having company this evening and *my* medicine was going to be due right about the time they were coming. And if *I* was going to run out of steam right about the time of dinner...well, then *I* would plan better."

Pete said nothing. I was frustrated. I had no answers. I didn't know what to do about our plans for the evening.

I threw up my hands (always the flair for drama) and said, "That's it, I'm calling off our dinner plans."

"No, don't. I'll be alright. I'm gonna rest and then I'll be alright," he said.

"You know," I ramped up my argument, "the more you ignore this thing, MS, the more crazed I will get because you know, THIS IS A THING! (pause) IT'S A THING! And you trying to pretend it's not a thing just makes me more and more insane. Because IT'S A THING."

Still nothing. Pete was sitting on the side of the bed looking at me. Listening to me. He didn't know what to say. But I knew what I wanted him to say. I wanted him to admit that his body was failing, his mind was failing. I wanted him to articulate that this "thing" that was happening to us was multiple sclerosis. I wanted him to somehow remind me that his body was attacking itself and his nervous system was compromised. The signals from his brain that told him to use his core muscles or lift his legs weren't getting to his core or his legs. I wanted him to remind me of the unknown nature of this disease. I wanted him to own the fact that he didn't take his medication on time and that he needed rest. And I wanted him to remind me that on another day this same series of events might very well have produced a different result.

I wanted him to speak sense into my interrogation. He knew better than anyone else how fickle and capricious MS was. I wished he would reason with my unreasonable line of questioning. I needed him to sit with me and acknowledge that we could not control what was happening. I wanted to interrogate and reason together. He wanted to take his meds and take a nap so he would be ready for our company.

In concession, I asked, "Do you need anything else in order for you to rest?"

"My meds and a glass of water," he said.

I huffed myself to the bathroom, found his meds, filled a glass with water and brought them out to Pete. He reached for the meds, threw them in his mouth, reached for the cup, spilled some on himself while getting it to his mouth. He handed me the cup back and asked me to help him sit up. I helped. He sat up, swallowed some water then laid back down to get some rest.

Once I got him settled, I went downstairs, folded myself onto the couch and cried.

My mind still didn't give up its need to question. Why couldn't he move his legs this time? What was going on? Why was this happening today? Would the medicine really work? Was that what this was about? Why does it seem like this happens whenever we made plans?

I took a deep breath through my nose and I said aloud, "I hate MS."

Yes, I hated MS.

THE GIFT OF CONFESSION

MY GREAT AUNT DIED THE DAY AFTER CHRISTMAS. She was 89 years old. She spoke five languages, taught each of us to play the piano and was an avid reader and thinker. She was actually my grandmother's best friend and not really my aunt, although we spent every holiday with her. She used to give me gift certificates to McDonald's for Christmas. This Christmas she gave me the gift of "confession." On Christmas morning my mother called to say that Aunt Lea had been rushed to the hospital and the doctor didn't think she would live through the hour. I found my aunt barely alive. She had fallen the night before. She was anemic, indicating that there was internal bleeding. The fall had set off a series of events that were unrecoverable. Her physician explained our options with tremendous skill, caring for her body and soul. The decision to stop treatment was not difficult and yet it was the largest decision I had ever been part of.

She was in and out of consciousness and therefore aware of the decision we needed to make. We believed that she understood her options. She would wake and look to my mom or me for information. We would say again, "Aunt Lea, you're very sick. There are some things that they can do but no one believes they will help. There is bleeding. Do you understand?" She would nod. "We don't believe there is anything that they can do." A nod. "That means that you're dying." To that, she said, "Everyone must die."

I chuckled a little when she said that. She was so matter-of-fact. Of course,she was right. "Yes, Aunt Lea," I said, "you're right. Everyone must die." And then I put my face really close to hers and said, "I love you, Aunt Lea." She said she loved me too. And then I said, "Aunt Lea, I'm sorry that I didn't practice the piano more." What? What was wrong with me? Why did it matter that I hadn't practiced the piano? Why was that so important to confess?

I worried that I might have failed her in some way. It's possible that when I was in the fourth grade she really would have liked to see me practice more. Go ahead and laugh; I did.

I don't wish that I hadn't said it. Instead I wish that I had said it before that day. I wish that I, broken, fragile and human, had talked to her about practicing and about how hard it was and is. I wish that I had more time to talk to her about what was important to her. It wasn't about practicing the piano, every fourth grader I knew hated to practice the piano. It was about who I was and whether she loved me as I was. And then of course it is whether I was ok with who I was.

Had I done enough? As a young piano student? As her niece? Ultimately, was I enough?

This question of being enough was an underlying question of caregiving. Was I doing enough? Had I done enough? Was I enough?

I never asked, but I did wonder whether people around me believed that I was doing my very best. I thought I was. I wondered if anyone wished I was caring for Pete better than I was. The truth was, I wasn't sure if I would ever be able to care for Pete as well as I wished he was cared for. I struggled with caring for his needs. I struggled with my patience and compassion every day.

I wished that I was enough. I wished that I was enough of a niece to my sweet Aunt Lea, enough of a pastor to my congregation, enough of a wife to Pete. It wasn't about what Aunt Lea thought or didn't think of me. And it wasn't about what my congregation thought or even what Pete thought. This was a personal problem. I needed to believe I was enough. I needed to believe that when we chose one another, whether in the covenant of marriage or within the companionship of community, we were enough. I needed to stop wanting to be more than I was able to be. I needed to accept my fragility, my mortality, my brokenness.

I needed to stop climbing that bizarre staircase in my dream thinking that I could find a better way to live my life. I was grasping for answers or for better tools. I needed to go to back down those stairs and realize that second guessing myself, or shaming myself was essentially facing the wrong direction. I needed to accept my fragile, mortal, broken self and live my life as it was unfolding. I wasn't meant to suffer through life, to struggle through life. I was meant to live my life as it was. I was enough.

TRUEST PRAYER

I HAVE READ C.S. LEWIS' *TIL WE HAVE FACES* about six times. The culminating meaning for me is found in this paragraph.

...to say the very thing you really mean, the whole of it, nothing more or less or other than what you really mean; that's the whole art and joy of words... When the time comes to you at which you will be forced at last to utter the speech which has lain at the center of your soul for years, which you have, all that time, idiot-like, been saying over and over, you'll not talk about joy of words. I saw well why the gods do not speak to us openly, nor let us answer. Till that word can be dug out of us, why should they hear the babble that we think we mean? How can they meet us face to face till we have faces?[5]

I had just finished reading this lesser known novel by Lewis. I was sitting on my porch drinking iced tea. I laid aside my book and took a deep breath and faced God as directly as I knew how. A prayer emerged from within me. It was if it had been excavated from somewhere deep in my soul. It was spontaneous, honest, without pretense or burden, without agenda or obligation. I wrote these words down:

My soul hushes.
My core tightens.
My head tilts back.
I smile and say
thank you.

Those words, this prayer feels
different than any other.
Years of study. Piles of books.

---

[5] Lewis, C.S. *Til We Have Faces,* Harper One, 2017, page 335.

Floods of thoughts.
I had wrestled with God
but had never
sat face to face.

God was much larger than I had imagined.

And all I really had to say
was
Thank you.

The only action
a smile.
Yet hope and faith,
wonder and dismay,
fed that smile.
Yes hope and faith,
wonder and dismay
removed the veil
I had being wearing.

Without a veil, my feelings
were laid bare.
I saw my face; I saw me.

It's not God's face that struck me.
It was my own.
Face to face with God, and
my own face was the one
about which I was learning.

My face was thankful,
grateful,
remarkably small and humble.

I did not linger with my face.
I was exposed and afraid
my truest self was thankful.

SACRED SPACE

I RECEIVED A CALL FROM AN ELDER at a neighboring church asking if I would come pray with them. His church was in transition and he and his family found themselves without a pastor. His daughter, Anne, was about to lose her husband, Joe to cancer. Joe was 36 years old.

I arrived at Anne's house and walked through the kitchen door where the first wafting smell hit me. "It smells amazing in here." Anne's mother said, "We baked a pie." If only pie could fix everything. Anne's mother, Anne's father, and Anne were all squished in the galley-sized kitchen, taking a break from the heartache and taking in the smell of pie. I gave everyone a hug and then came back around to Anne.

I put my arm around her to hold her for awhile. I looked up to all three of them and said, "Tell me what's happening now."

"We needed a break."

"It's so hard to watch."

"This isn't how it's supposed to be."

"This wasn't the plan."

I nodded after each response and then said to Anne, "Come on, introduce me to Joe."

On the way to the bedroom, we passed a dozen family members. Some were watching the Giants game. Some were staring into space. Some were playing with her son, Domani, on the floor. The house was full, and not just of people. The house was full of thoughts and emotions and confusion. The house was full of relationships and love. The house was full of grief and sickness and thoughts of the future.

Joe was in a hospital bed in the guest room of their home. An additional twin bed lay beside him where Anne slept at night. The hospice nurse was sitting on the extra twin, keeping written accounts of his breathing. At the foot of his bed, there was a 37-

inch flat screen tv, also playing the Giants game. I introduced myself to Joe and reached for his hand with my right and took Anne's hand with my left.

And then an odd thing happened. It was as if Anne "left the room." She leaned over to brush his hair. She swallowed a tear. And then she came back.

She never left in her physical body, of course, but a distance emerged between us, even as I held her hand. It felt as if she and Joe were sneaking a few moments together in a space closest to their hearts, through a door to which we, meaning me, the hospice nurse, his family, did not have a key. They had found a way, or at least Anne had found a way, to be alone with him despite the pervasive presence of others.

I turned to the hospice nurse and asked about his breathing. She told me when his last breath was. His breathing was shallow and the space between breaths was increasing. I looked up to see that his mother and father were standing just outside the doorway. Although divorced, they were consoling and supporting one another. Joe's father's grief was overflowing onto his ex-wife.

"Come in; join us," I said. When they were around the bed, I released Joe's hand to touch his parents. Touch. I had no words. My currency was touch.

I turned to Joe and said, "Joe, I thought I'd say a prayer. Your parents are here with Anne and me."

I looked up to find everyone's eyes and I reached out for us to hold hands. We created a circle of sacred space around a fragile, dying young man. I gave thanks for the richness of life and the faithfulness of love that had created this sacred circle. I spoke about the fleeting and labored breath that we have in this life. I gave thanks for how precious our life is because of the love we have here and now. I gave thanks for family and for love and for memories. I gave thanks for this specific moment in time, holding hands around his bed together. And I gave thanks for the strength and courage that helps us walk, stumble, or crawl through loss. I gave thanks for the life of the person who made this circle possible. "Thank you, God, for Joe's life."

But what words did I have for the life that would not be

lived, the love that would not be given, the steps that would not be taken? I paused. I took a deep breath and I spoke the truth, "God, we don't understand. We don't like this. We are hurting and we need your help. And we even wonder where you are." And then I paused again and took another breath and reminded myself and those praying with me, "with every touch and every breath, God is with us. God is in us. God is around us. God is beneath us. God is here. God lives through us. God touches us when we touch one another."

I have a plaque in my office: "Vocatus atque non vocatus deus aderit." It is a Latin saying of Erasmus that Carl Jung popularized. It translates: Bidden or Not, God is present. Called or not, God is present. Summoned or not summoned, God is present. Invoked or not invoked, God is present. For us, holding hands in a circle around Joe's bed, with the Giants playing in the background, God was with us.

GOD'S JOB DESCRIPTION

WHEN WE WERE LOOKING FOR A NEW PLACE TO LIVE we put a bid on a place and didn't get it. I remember calling my mother to let her know we didn't get it, and she quickly gave me a pep talk saying, "When I pray for you, I know that God has you covered." My mother wanted me to rely on God saying, "You've gotta simply trust the Lord for this. God is in this. I'm sure of it." She told me to go home, take Pete's hand, and then she quoted the Bible saying, "Present your requests to God with thanksgiving."

When I told my dad that we didn't get the condo, he also began a pep talk; it was a little shorter but still a pep talk. He said, "Honey. God has another plan." I remember saying to both of them that I simply didn't have the faith for this line of thinking right now but I was happy for them to believe for me.

There was another condo in the same development, the same layout but they were looking to sell, not rent. We could never afford to purchase this home. Our realtor reached out and asked if they would be interested in renting. They offered a one-year lease to us. One year seemed horribly unpredictable. My friend Linda expressed concern that a one-year lease only introduced an additional unknown. She told me my life was already filled with unpredictability, I didn't need to worry about where we would live in 12 months. I responded, "Maybe the lesson in this for me is to learn to live one day at a time." I barely got the sentence out and she cut me off saying, "God has already taught you that lesson. You're living that lesson with Pete's illness. Every day was already unpredictable."

All of us: My mother, my father, my friend, and me, each in our own way was asserting that God had some interest in my life, in how I was living with Pete's illness and even in finding us a new home. Even though I was trying to make my life have meaning with each twist and turn, I didn't really believe that finding me a new place to live was in God's job description. In fact, if finding me a house was on God's "to do" list, we all had much bigger problems.

Multiple choice: One of the tasks on God's job description is:

A. Protecting children from the sex trade
B. Feeding the hungry
C. Preventing tsunamis
D. Finding Beth and Pete a new home within their time frame and price range
E. None of the above

At the time, I believed the correct answer was E. None of the Above. Why? Because it doesn't seem as though A through C were getting done and they were categorically more important than D. How about this question: True or False: If any of A through D were on God's job description, God needed to be fired for gross negligence. My answer? True.

Somewhere along the way, I had misunderstood God's job description. And I was reevaluating my understanding of God, of us, of our world. There was something about living with a progressive disease, facing challenge after challenge, that had me understanding God as perhaps a little less involved with our lives than I had once thought. And the more I experienced hurt, trauma, grief, in my own life and in the lives of those in my congregation, I entertained the idea that God didn't seem to be fixing many of the problems in the world. And if I were to list the problems in the world, neither Pete's diagnosis nor our need for a new condo was a top priority. If I were to triage the needs in the world, if it was my job to set God's agenda, I believe I would make sure protecting widows and orphans, creating safe living space for refugees, keeping women from being abused, ceasing wars based on religious ideology, and preventing super powers from controlling the world's economy were higher on the list than finding Beth and Pete a new home. But it appeared God was not doing any of those things. And when I read the prophets of old, it appeared God wasn't doing any of those things back then either.

Rather than send God packing for gross negligence, I was willing to accept that I had clearly misunderstood her job description. So I backed my thinking up a step—I don't employ God. Rather, God employs me.

So again, the answer really was E. "None of the above" was on God's job description. I needed to stop holding God accountable for things not on her job description. I could stop being angry at God for not doing what she was supposed to do—because she wasn't supposed to be doing those things in the first place.

Don't get me wrong. I was still hurt, and I was grieving those things left undone, but I started to imagine that God was also hurt too. God was grieving that which was not done. Rather than approach God with gnawing irritation or indignation over how God was somehow not caring for me and Pete and the problems associated with MS, I started to sense God was right beside me, right with us on this horrible journey of loss after loss after loss.

God was not going to fix this; God was not going to heal Pete. But God still was. And if God still was, then I wanted a relationship with God. It would be a different relationship for God was not who I had thought God was. For me, not blaming God for things that God wasn't supposed to do was a first step toward establishing an appropriate relationship with God. I would have to get to know who God was as if meeting God for the first time.

If this were a possibility, I'd want to meet at a diner for breakfast. I imagine God already sitting in a booth and drinking coffee. I would begin with, "So God, where you from?" If I were writing the script, God would say, "I come from before." I'd nod and wonder, "What the hell does that mean?" And then I'd wonder, "What the hell do I say to that?" Despite my internal monologue, I would continue because I am tenacious. "So what's your favorite color? Oh no, let me guess. It's green, right?" God would respond, "No, Beth, that's your favorite color. But have you considered that the way that you see green is not the way that I see green?" I'm thrilled that my tea has arrived and I look God right in the face (not quite sure what God's face would look like) and I would say, "In fact, I have considered that."

Clearly, I didn't think that God is a great conversationalist. And so asking God to help me understand God's job description was probably not going to get me very far, so I was still left wondering what was on God's job description because I had ruled out the sex trade, hunger, tsunamis and finding me a new home. Perhaps I shouldn't worry so much about God's job description but instead worry about my own. What was my job here on earth? For that I turned to the prophet Micah who asked the question "What does the Lord require of you?" and then answered his own question saying "to do justice, and to love kindness, and to walk humbly." (Micah 6:8)

Job Title: Human Being

Objective: Do justice, Love kindness, Walk humbly with God

So, it turns out that some of the things that I thought were on God's job description were actually on mine. Protecting widows and orphans, creating safe places for refugees, keeping women from being abused, ceasing wars based on religious ideology, preventing super powers from controlling the world's economy... Mercy!

Suddenly I imagined that conversation with God going very differently. Suddenly I wanted to listen to what God wanted me to do. I jokingly assumed that God was not a good conversationalist. But the truth was, I was either too busy talking or too frustrated to listen. What if God was always trying to talk to us about what to do? What if we were receiving instructions for everything we saw and heard? What if we perceived God as uninterested because God wasn't doing what we wanted God to do? What if God wasn't less involved in our lives? What if instead God was so very near to our lives, right beside us, whispering to us instructions on how to heal the wounds of the world?

In fact, I think that's what my mom was getting at when I first told her about being outbid on the condo. She wanted Pete and me to hold each other's hands and to "present our requests to God with thanksgiving." But she didn't finish the Bible quote. The end of the verse says, "and *the peace of God, which passes all understanding, will guard our hearts and minds*." (Philippines 4:7)

When I talked to God, God offered peace. When we came near enough to God to talk, we discovered God was near enough to us—to talk to us and to listen to us and to be with us. Ultimately, God offers peace that guards our hearts and minds.

Our job: Talk to God and to one another, and be thankful.

God's job: Offer peace.

I confess that I didn't go home and take Pete's hand and say a prayer. Instead I went home and snuggled on the couch with him and asked, "What is it that you really want in a house?" And we talked. And I believed that God was with us. Without knowing where our next home would be, we had peace. It passed our understanding. And this peace guarded our hearts and minds while we waited for the right place to live.

I Like to Be Ready

SUPERSTORM SANDY RAVAGED A PATH UP THE EASTERN COAST, forcing waves beyond the boardwalk. Millions of people in New Jersey were left without power. Thirty miles north in the stairwells of a New York City hospital, nurses carried patients to safety because the generator failed. They were ready. They had a plan and a backup plan. Both plans failed.

I have always liked being ready. I wouldn't say I plan ahead but rather I live ahead. I have a hard time living in the present; I prefer the future. I constantly imagine and adjust for life ahead of where I actually am. I have been known to confuse that with being ready.

Before the storm I was at the grocery store buying junk food and eggs. Everyone else was buying water and batteries. I had not considered purchasing batteries as a sign of readiness.

Being ready sounds like a great idea. But so many of the important things in life are really impossible to get ready for. For example, I imagined being a stepmother, but I couldn't have been ready for how two young men stole my heart. I imagined the day Dan got married, but I was shocked by how important his wife Faith was in my life. I imagined a baby in our family, but I was not ready for how the center of gravity shifted with her arrival. I had imagined and promised to love someone in sickness and in health, but I was not ready for disability to upend my life. When Pete was diagnosed with MS, I tried to imagine caring for him but I was not ready for the volume of compassion required, nor for the impatience I could generate. I could imagine living with love, but I was not ready to fear love because of loss.

So while the wind of the storm howled around us, we cuddled with our junk food and I admitted to Pete, "I wasn't ready for you to use a wheelchair. I wasn't ready."

A few days earlier Pete had agreed to accept the gift of a hand-me-down motorized wheelchair. Jean, the woman in my congregation who passed away from ALS, left her motorized wheelchair to her friends at our church to pass on as they saw fit. For the past few years, a young man in our community, also with ALS, had used it. He had recently passed away. And the wheelchair became available. Those same friends approached Pete to see if he would like to use it. He said yes. I was shocked.

In the past Pete had been slow to accept his limitations of his disease. He put off trying new assistive devices because he was avoiding or delaying or denying what was happening to him. For him to say to yes to this device told me that his ability to walk was much worse than any of us knew it was. It also told me that he was ready to be a "wheeling" person rather than a "walking" person. This seemed like such a large jump. I was surprised.

He was ready but I was not. As many times as I had complained (sometimes only to myself) about having to walk slower beside him, I still preferred to walk slowly beside him than to walk beside a person scooting along in a motorized wheelchair. I wasn't ready.

There was no planning for what lies ahead. No one was able to tell us what the trajectory of the disease was for Pete. No one was able to tell us the slope of the progression or the speed of the slope. There was no way to be ready for what was happening to him, to me, to us. And even if we could be ready, plans of readiness fail all the time—like the generator at that hospital in New York.

As the wind howled around us, as we waited to see the damage that had happened along the Jersey coast, the storm was speaking to me saying, "Whatever you do. You cannot prepare for what will be." One of my favorite poems by Rainer Maria Rilke begins,

You are not surprised by the force of the storm
you have seen it coming. [6]

There had been times in my life when I saw the storm coming. Times when I felt a change afoot. Events and information warned me to expect change. But there was no way to be ready for the "storm" called multiple sclerosis.

---

[6] Rilke, Rainer Maria, et al. *Rilke's Book of Hours: Love Poems to God.* Riverhead Books, 2005.

ADJUSTMENTS

WE NEEDED A NEW CAR. Not just any new car, we needed a mini-van that had been converted to accommodate a motorized wheelchair. Pete and I had never been new car people. We had bought used cars and then drove them until they owed us nothing. We had driven cars until they were ready to be donated to a friend or a good cause. When I donated my first car, a white Chevy Beretta, my siblings came over for pancakes and we watched it towed away. We even shed a few tears. We had been through several cars since then.

I was driving Pete's Honda CR-V that had 140K miles on it. Pete had already given up driving. With a manual wheelchair, Pete transferred from wheelchair to the passenger seat. Then the wheelchair was stored in the back, and we were on our way. The downside for me was the time it took to assist Pete into the car and lifting the wheelchair into the back.

A motorized wheelchair was a whole different thing. A motorized wheelchair uses a ramp to get into the vehicle and then depending on the style, the wheelchair takes up the passenger seat or one of the back seats. We had rented a handicap accessible vehicle for a doctor's appointment once. In that case the wheelchair was one of the middle seats in the mini-van. As we talked about our needs, we hoped for as much autonomy and independence we could afford. So we headed back to the same mobility center to shop for a van. We met with Diane—a cheerful, honest woman who worked regularly with people with disabilities. How did I know that? She faced and talked to Pete the whole time. She walked slower. She offered help by saying, "If you need help, just holler," instead of hovering or assuming. I was still learning that lesson. She was a pro.

Buying a converted mini-van is like purchasing two cars: the car and then the conversion. We were shocked at the sticker price. A new converted mini-van was $70K. They had a few used ones on the lot. We test drove a dark red 2002 Chevy and a silver 2002 Chrysler, both with 60K miles on them. Each of them were around $22K. That was better than $70K.

Pete got in and out of each, checked out how the locking features worked, and we were pretty settled on the Chrysler, I thought. But then we debriefed on the ride home. Pete made an innocent comment about still being able to transfer to the passenger seat. He said, "We could wheel me up to this van, I could transfer to the passenger seat and then we could store the wheelchair in the back." I totally lost my cool. I said, "That's what we do now! Why do we need a new car then?"

I was so confused at the adjustments we were making, or rather he was making. He was ready to have a motorized wheelchair but then still wanted to use a manual wheelchair when we left the house? I couldn't possibly understand how hard this was for him to navigate. He was certainly coming to grips with his mobility issues. He was coming up against his limitations and trying to figure out how to adjust. I was trying to keep up with his decisions. He now had a motorized wheelchair and we no longer had a vehicle to accommodate said motorized wheelchair. I thought I was adjusting.

A new home, a new wheelchair, a new car. I didn't ask for any of these changes. I didn't want any of this. And I really didn't want to be the one who had to argue for Pete's needs to Pete himself! I tried to explain the disconnect that was happening. But we were missing each other.

When I told my friends this story they were faithful to remind me that what Pete and I were going through was a big deal. "These type of adjustments are not easy," they said. I heard them...sort of. I understood all the words, but I still questioned what about these adjustments was so difficult. I mean, people buy cars all the time. People rent condos all the time. Making changes doesn't have to include lengthy, heated discussions trying to get on the same page as your partner, does it? Why couldn't we adjust with more ease? Why couldn't we just drop the extra baggage of MS and make changes for the love of God.

Deeper down, I knew my friends were right. We were going through a big deal, a host of big deals actually. The van we needed wasn't just any van The van we looked at literally "knelt" to us when the ramp opened. And the condo we needed wasn't just another condo either. Our building had an elevator that went to a parking garage. And there was no one in our building anywhere close to my age because it was an age 55 and older community. We chose this community because it provided all of the things Pete needed. All of the adjustments we were making were in response to multiple sclerosis. We couldn't negotiate any of these changes without thinking of, considering, kneeling to the needs of multiple sclerosis. It was as if the disease was a third party in our negotiations. No wonder we were taking longer to adjust.

Mild Pain
Versus Moderate Pain

PETE HAD SERVED AS A DEACON AT OUR CHURCH for most of the time I had worked there. Along with his fellow Deacons, he had visited the sick, the hurting, and the lonely. They made friends with the friendless. They prayed for and with people. Their currency was meaningful touches and smiles. They worked hard and faced difficult situations together. And when they got together at their monthly meeting, they laughed hard. They knew that facing sadness together would also require laughter and friendship.

On the way to one of their meetings, Pete asked me, "How would you differentiate between 'mild pain' and 'moderate pain'?" I answered, "Mild pain requires no medical attention. Moderate pain, to me, would make me want to speak to a professional." "Hmmm," he said.

I waited, for certainly there was more. Finally, I broke the silence and asked him, "How would *you* differentiate between "mild pain" and "moderate pain?" He provided a short answer, "I find the two words to be synonymous."

Again, I waited for a follow-up comment. Fifteen years of marriage, and I was still waiting for a comment when one was not coming. "Why do you ask?" I say.

"Oh, I read something today and it got me thinking," he said.

"How did the article differentiate between between mild and moderate pain?" I asked.

"Well, you know, they agree with you. But I still don't see the difference in the two words."

"Well, if the article agrees with me, then don't you think perhaps physicians would agree with me too. And then you should perhaps adopt these definitions particularly if a physician is asking you if you're to tell them whether you are or were in mild or moderate pain?"

"But I'm not in any pain. So I don't need to describe pain to anyone," Pete said

"Well then why are we talking about this?"

"Because I read something..."

I never knew what Pete was going to talk about. This was one of the reasons why I loved him so. He wanted to read anything, discuss anything. And he had such different perspectives than I did. His mind would forever be different than mine, and trying always to stay on top of everything, understand everything was such a waste of my time. And trying to get him to agree that mild pain was not the same as moderate pain was really a waste of time. He thought what he thought, and I thought what I thought, and getting frustrated by not understanding was such a waste of my time.

Instead we laughed at one another; we laughed at our differences. By the time we walked into the meeting, Pete and I were laughing and arguing about the difference between mild and moderate pain combined with the difference between how his and my brain functioned. I was mildly irritated by the fact that he would not accept my answer as reasonable. Mild and moderate pain were the same thing, he maintained.

We were a little punchy and the Deacons loved us for it. I decided to ask what their thoughts were about mild and moderate pain. To Pete's surprise, most folks agreed with me. And yet... he remained unmoved in his opinion.

Pete sat down at the table, and I noticed he was slouching a little bit, and I started to ask him whether he wouldn't be more safe in a chair that had armrests, but I decided that a question like that was close to asking if I could help without being asked in the first place. So, I let it go. He could take care of himself. If he needed a different chair he would ask for it. We settled ourselves around a folding table littered with paper, pens, and snacks.

Thirty minutes later Pete fell off the chair. He leaned over and just kept going. His arms didn't react to catch himself. His legs didn't seem to flinch in order to brace for impact. He just fell over. His core muscles stopped getting the signal to hold him upright.

We were in a room full of compassionate people and everyone jumped to help—but Pete stopped us in our tracks. Using his sternest voice, he said, "Nobody move." We all froze and we quietly watched him as he moved to pick himself up. Everyone wanted to respond. Everyone was concerned. Everyone loved Pete. But the really interesting thing was I didn't think any of us were surprised. How were we not surprised by Pete falling off a chair? It wasn't like people fell off chairs all the time in the middle of meetings! Yet somehow, we had all grown accustomed to odd, unpredictable things happening with Pete. We had somehow accepted the relentless unpredictability of multiple sclerosis.

The folks around this table had been with us since the beginning of his diagnosis. They knew our everyday life; they prayed for our every moment worries. They were aware of medication changes and doctor's reports. They had collected stories about Pete. They each had their own experiences with Pete. We all knew there was one thing we could expect—the unexpected. With a chronic illness as unpredictable as multiple sclerosis, everything in life turned out to be a surprise, so in turn most things stopped surprising us.

So Pete was lying on the floor, working his way to a seated position. We were all waiting for directions about how we might be helpful. Pete looked up at us, took a breath and said, "This is what I call mild pain."

Laughter. Lots of laughter.

Pete and I, and all of these Deacons, had chosen to live in community. Choosing life in community has meant that we experience life exponentially. Together we had experienced that many more births, that many more deaths, that many more weddings, that many more illnesses and surgeries, and that much more laughter. Choosing community had meant learning so much more. We had been exposed to so much more.

Pete and I had made these promises to one another: to have and hold, to love and cherish…in sickness and in health. Pete and I had made promises to this community as well: to support one another, nurture one another, serve one another. We promised to worship together and to work together. Just as in marriage, we had no idea what we're getting into!

I was grateful for that group of people who had witnessed our lives that evening. I was grateful for how they entertained our conversation about pain. I was grateful for their kindness and patience and even their lack of surprise at having watched Pete fall over. I was grateful for their laughter. When I was falling asleep later that evening, I was grateful that Pete and I were not alone in life. Our lives were out of our control and there were others who were willing, even eager to be in life with us.

Epilogue:
The Last Dance

PETE AND I WERE SITTING ON THE SHORELINE OF CAPE COD. I had just officiated a wedding in which the congregation sat in plastic white chairs facing the water. The newly married couple took their first steps together in an Orthodox ring ceremony where rocky beach and the grassy lawn met. The bridal party had just finished taking pictures and we were waiting for a golf cart to pick us up. Pete was still using a walker at this point. His gait was often wobbly. Earlier in the day, someone had tried to help us open the door and when Pete turned to thank the person, he lost his footing and fell. So the staff were being extra cautious with him, for which we were grateful. But this extra caution was running 45 minutes behind schedule. And so there Pete and I sat, all dressed up, debriefing the wedding, and enjoying the shoreline of Cape Cod. Water, birds, and the distant sound of a wedding reception getting underway.

The bride was a dear friend. She was my first yoga teacher. Her betrothed was a hopeful actor. During the reception I was to lead the couple in a "common cup ceremony," a tradition of the Greek Orthodox church. The bride's family was of Greek origin. Pete and I had chosen a clay mug from a local artisan to use for the ceremony.

Finally, the cavalry arrived, we zoomed up the hill and around the sidewalks, where we were delivered to the reception. Pete and I found our way to our table and introduced ourselves to our dinner mates. Once Pete was settled, I headed over to the bride and groom, mug in hand. They opened their gift, smiled at the artistry, and the thoughtfulness of adapting the ancient ceremony. I went to the DJ to get a microphone to begin the reception with this ceremony.

As best as I can remember, I said something like "in the gospel of John there is a story about Jesus turning water to wine. In this common cup ceremony, I pour wine into the cup and ask the bride and groom to drink from the same cup. By doing so, they begin their journey together, drinking in the water of life and the wine of life, the joy and the sorrows of life, all in one cup."

I suppose this is the Greek Orthodox way of saying what Pete always says, "you pay one price, you go on all the rides." Our marriage license had cost us $28. We split it and then we were forever able to say, "Hey, listen. I paid $14 for that." We paid $14 for that argument. We paid $14 for that kiss. We paid $14 to squeeze each other's butt. We paid $14 and we were entitled to go on every ride. Pay one price; go on all the rides.

This ride with multiple sclerosis was not very fun. We said that fairly often. But the truth remained—we paid one price; we were going to go on all the rides…together.

When the common cup ceremony was complete I headed back over to Pete. I held out my hand, and asked him to dance. We loved to dance. And in our case, dancing was less an active sport and more a daily practice of holding one another and swaying. Most every day for our marriage, Pete had come home from work and found me, most of the time in the kitchen preparing dinner. He reached out to find my waist or my hands and pulled me close enough to sway and turn for two minutes, three at the most. His right hand on the small of my back, my right hand in his left. We needed no music for this daily practice. We were the music. Our inside lives were the rhyme and our outside lives were the rhythm. We danced to the daily "ride," whatever it was.

On the dance floor at that wedding, I recall my right hand in his and his right hand on my waist, but both of us were holding on tighter. More of his weight was in my arms. And his walker, which had a chair rest on it, was right beside us, just in case we needed it. This dance, which would turn out to be our last, was more swaying and less turning. I don't recall the song. But I remember we made it through about half of it before he needed to take a break. We happily headed over to our table to enjoy the evening, to breathe in the decadence of celebrating the promises that had been made.

We never knew when the last dance would happen. The "last" was never announced. The last day with a walking stick. The last day with a walker. The last day at work. The last day driving. The last day before a diagnosis with MS. "Lasts" happened all the time Loss happened all the time. Grief, loss, faith, and doubt happened all the time and they mingled into a tangled dance of swaying and turning.

My daughter-in-law told me that Pete had told her the one thing he missed the most was dancing with me. I'm not sure what I missed the most since we had been on this "ride" with multiple sclerosis. We had both lost a lot. Certainly his losses were more profound. Whatever I lost, Pete's losses were harder to accept. Maybe I had to change my plans for the day. But Pete couldn't move his legs for that day. So in the grand scheme of things, I have not felt entitled to name what I miss the most.

Perhaps I can't name my greatest loss because loss for me came in a series of little losses. The great loss for me was how they all just kept coming. It was the long, slippery slope that was our life those first seven years. Doctors would describe the trajectory of secondary progressive MS to us by saying it is a continuous, downward slope but we don't know the angle. We don't know how steep the slope is. For Pete, the slope was actually not steep. He had this disease for 25 years before diagnosis. It was a shallow slope. But by the time he was diagnosed, the ride had gained some momentum. It was moving faster and faster. One loss led to another and then another and I never felt like I got my footing. I felt like we were always adjusting to something new, always behind the curve.

As we have walked this downward slope together, not just Pete and I but our friends, our family, our church community, I did not ask God, "Why?" I did not believe God caused Pete's illness. I believed instead God has given us life, a miraculous existence, with waterproof skin, an internal cooling system, a hard drive to beat all hard drives. God made us good, very good, in fact. And I also believed our planet was constantly changing. Everything about our world was fighting to live and sometimes when one thing lives, another thing dies.

And where I had seen forces in our world fighting, overtly and covertly, internally and externally, I had also seen forces in our world loving one another, overtly and covertly, internally and externally. Love is a force to be reckoned with. Holding hands heals. Standing in solidarity is a super power. Praying for one another, with words or in silence, diminishes pain. Sharing a meal creates community and community offers God's presence right here in our world. I didn't need to ask where God was or is in this life because I knew who God was. God was living and breathing in people around me, the ones I knew and the ones I didn't. God was the person who packed my groceries at the grocery store. God walked beside me on my way to the public library. God drove the car that let me into traffic on my way to the hospital. God was with me, as surely as there were others around me.

I definitely get that folks have preferred God to show up in more supernatural ways. People have prayed for God to fix it, to change it, to heal, to mend. People have wanted God to eradicate pain, war, famine, illness, poverty. And so God answered us by giving us the ability to eradicate pain, war, famine, illness and poverty. God has always been very present. The Christian scriptures say, "God is love." It is not that God is loving...no, the Christian scriptures say God is love itself.

God gave us the ability to love—in sickness and in health. Who was God when I hurt? God was the one who loved us, in sickness and in health. God was the one who stayed beside us, and looked exactly like our close friends, our neighbors, and our church family. God was the one who didn't shy away from my tears. God was the one who held my hand. God was the one who made sense of medical bills. God was the one with the stethoscope. God was the pharmacist who asked the best questions. God was the dance of my closest girlfriends as they packed up my kitchen, having to move when I didn't want to. God was the dance of my congregation who embraced Pete with a walking stick, a walker, a rollator and eventually a wheelchair. I didn't have to ask "where was God?" because I knew who to look for when I needed God the most.

ACKNOWLEDGMENTS

My late husband reminded us as often as he could that "we live with an embarrassment of blessings." Indeed, that is true all the time but particularly in how this book has come to fruition.

This book had it genesis when Dr. Virginia Wiles, one of the many faithful seminary professor from New Brunswick Theological Seminary, trusted a voice in me that I did not know at the time. For her bold encouragement to cultivate and write in this voice, I am so deeply grateful. The second encouragement came through a faithful church woman (in this book you will find that some of the most faithful, fierce women in the world are those who sit in the pews of a church), Laura Peterson, who read the first manuscript that ended after seminary graduation. She encouraged me to write through the first year of my pastorate. Of course, neither of us would know my husband would be diagnosed with MS that first year, or that this book would become an altogether different piece of work. But her wisdom to keep listening to my life and to broaden my own discussion was golden.

There are many other people I would like to acknowledge. Carol Howard Merritt, a friend, cheerleader, and guide who once handed me a slip of paper that said, 'this is your year." I kept that slip of paper in clear sight for several years as I wrote and rewrote, prayed, and cried through many of the stories in this memoir. Carol, you are a blessing to so many. Through Carol's ability to cultivate community I met Doug Hagler, colleague and friend, who read this book before it had structure and heard the story I was meant to tell. For his belief in what could be, I give thanks.

I am grateful for the community at caregiver.com, and its founder, Denise Brown. When I was uncertain of speaking my truth, or when I was embarrassed of the level of vulnerability in my writing, I remembered that caregivers need one another to share the "real deal" lest we think we are alone. Caregivers and former caregivers and future caregivers: You are giants.

"Team Scibienski," in particular the physicians on our team, thank you for your works of kindness and discernment. Thank you for not only providing physical care for Pete, but also for appreciating his sense of humor and for honoring our questions. Your presence in my life enabled me to exhale in times of deep stress and sadness.

My editor, Karen Hodges Miller, and illustrator, Eric Labacz. Thank you for your encouragement on this first ride of publishing for me. I'm grateful for how you have escorted this story into its public life.

My family of origin, and those others who stood beside us as we got married, those who knew Pete and I as a couple before MS entered the scene, thank you for small acts of kindnesses and large acts of sacrifices. John and Linda, thank you for not being afraid of what was about to happen to Pete and me. Thank you for laughter. For loving Pete in your unique Pepe way. For the weekly gathering of the "sistas" who listened, laughed, cried, and prayed with me consistently. There are stories that did not make it into this book, but I have tremendous gratitude for how you hold them in trust for me.

For the saints at Grace Presbyterian, those past and those present, who watched Pete lose his mobility slowly over the span of 13 years. I'm more than grateful for you, I am proud of who we have been together. I'm indebted to how the Holy Spirit has worked in and among us to create community. I'm grateful for how our community informs my understanding of God, and how you have always been open to the unanswered questions of faith and life. May the Spirit continue to enliven you, hold you and change you.

My most intimate clan, Dan and Faith, Joe and Teal, Julia and Mateo, you loved your dad with honor and honesty, laughter and love. And you continue to love me just the same. Thank you for encouraging my vulnerability, trusting my voice, and believing that my story matters. With you, every day is "just another day in paradise."

ABOUT THE AUTHOR

Beth Scibienski is the pastor of Grace Presbyterian Church, a vibrant congregation in central New Jersey, who love, learn, and laugh together. She started working at Grace one month before her late husband was diagnosed with secondary progressive multiple sclerosis. She is also a Reiki master.

Beth has blogged extensively on grief and loss. Her lectionary reflections are featured on Textweek at Textweek.com and have been published in the *Abington Preaching Annual 2016*. She is the co-host of the Two Pastors' Podcast at http://twopastors.libsyn.com/.

Beth has two adult sons name Dan and Joe. Dan and his wife, Faith, have two children, Julia and Mateo. The Scibienski clan is smart and kind. They keep Beth's theology fresh and honest. Together they have navigated life with resilience and grace. She enjoys playing the guitar, singing, and cooking local vegetables from local farms.

Made in the USA
San Bernardino, CA
17 October 2018